PRAYING THE WAY

♦ REFLECTIONS ON THE ♦ STATIONS OF THE CROSS

Gloria Hutchinson

ST. ANTHONY MESSENGER PRESS

CINCINNATI, OHIO

Nihil Obstat: Rev. Arthur J. Espelage, O.F.M.
Rev. Ralph J. Lawrence

Imprimi Potest: Rev. John Bok, O.F.M.
Provincial

Imprimatur: +Carl K. Moeddel, V.G.
Archdiocese of Cincinnati
September 26, 1994

Unless otherwise indicated, Scripture citations are taken from the *New Revised Standard Version Bible*, copyright ©1989, by the Division of Christian Education of the National Council of Churches of Christ in the U.S.A. and used by permission. All rights reserved.

Cover photograph by Gene Plaisted, O.S.C.
Cover and book design by Mary Alfieri
ISBN 0-86716-212-0

Published by St. Anthony Messenger Press
Printed in the U.S.A.

To my mother,

Pearl Lamora Capone,

and to those who,
even now, are
nailed
to the
wood

Contents

INTRODUCTION

I haven't prayed the Stations of the Cross in church for several
years. In the eyes of some, that may disqualify me for the
present task. I am glad for those who can still "do the Stations"
in the traditional manner. But I cannot. Feelings of self-
consciousness and pietism creep in, turning prayer into a
distracted exercise period (walk, genuflect, stand, kneel, stand,
walk).

Anthony de Mello, S.J., would, I think, understand this
awkward place I'm in. He tells the story of a pious old man who
had been a model of devotional practice all his life. On his
eightieth birthday, the man prayed that God would reveal to
him why he, the faithful one, was still "poor as a church
mouse," while his worldly business partner was a towering
success.

Said the church mouse to the Lord of creation: "I do not ask
that he [the partner] be punished, for that would be unchristian.
But please tell me: Why, why, why have you let him prosper
and why do you treat me thus?" And God promptly replied,
"Because you are such a monumental bore!"

I sympathize with the old man, just as I empathized with
poor Salieri in the film *Amadeus*. Salieri set out to be a model
of devotion so that God might reward him with musical talent.
But he remains a humdrum composer while the coarse
profligate Wolfgang Amadeus Mozart is gifted with outlandish
genius. For all his good intentions, Salieri was a monumental
bore who never got beyond adolescence in his relationship with
God.

De Mello's commentary on the story "Meditations" points

out that the monastic rule is "Do not speak unless you can improve on the silence." To that he adds, "Might not the same be said of prayer?"[1]

For me, the Stations as I had always prayed them in church were no longer an improvement on silence. And if I did not yawn as I made my rounds from Pilate's platform to Joseph of Arimathea's tomb, the Lord surely did. It is a proof of his patience that he never once interrupted the ritual with a peremptory, "What do you think you are doing?"

I remember considering deeply what I was doing during a particular open air communal praying of the Way. That day the prayer sunk all the way to my roots, twining new connections between God's word in the Book and in the tangled lives of those who walked beside me.

The place: a hillside in Lourdes where life-sized figures cast in bronze played out the Passion in reverent silence.

The context: a Lenten pilgrimage of seriously ill and severely disabled Catholics, many of them young people, sponsored by the Lourdes Center in Boston.

The conditions: a demanding climb even for those of us who, by virtue of our able bodies, were chosen to companion the weak and wheelchair-bound.

The consequences: After an hour's climb and laborious descent, the parallel between Calvary past and present came clear. Those of us who got to be Simon or the anonymous woman we call Veronica knew how privileged we had been to serve the Christ beside us, diminished by leukemia, twisted by cerebral palsy, immobilized by multiple sclerosis. In their company, I knew I had prayed the Way.

That April day in Lourdes came back to me recently when I read of the "Way of the Cross/Way of Compassion" organized by the Center for Action and Contemplation in Albuquerque, New Mexico. Pilgrims gathered on Good Friday to "re-member

2

the suffering of the Body of Christ" by processing through the heart of the city.

They carried a large wooden cross and banners bearing messages of justice and peace. Before federal buildings and in public squares, they paused to reflect on the voices of today's crucified: the homeless, people with AIDS, abused children, derailed Vietnam veterans, victims of racism and violence. When they reached the Civic Plaza at three o'clock, they knew they had made the Way.

On a tour of Germany, Richard Rohr, O.F.M., founder of the Center for Action and Contemplation, noted: "The idea of doing the stations as a political act was picked up by the people in all the churches with great enthusiasm—except for some clerics who told us, 'You're pulling the people out of the Church.' "[2]

If we want the Way of the Cross to change us and our world, we need to pull ourselves out of the Church long enough to discover the prayer's political and communal implications. We can pray Mary's Magnificat every evening with devotion. But if we never hear it as a prophetic cry for justice, a call to action on behalf of the lowly, we stunt our spiritual growth and fail to embrace the cause of God's Reign.

We need to take time considering the Stations—alone or with a few others. Then we can move on to practicing the Way as a communal prayer of solidarity with those who bear Christ's wounds in their bodies, souls and psyches.

This book is intended to help readers—alone and together as families, spiritual friends or small faith communities— internalize the Way. Each chapter begins with a reflection (Our Way) from ordinary life—my own or that of someone who calls me to conversion. The original epigraphs (the quotation that begins the reflection) may cast a different light on the theme or hold a small candle to the reader's own experience. Question sections (Reflect) invite the reader to stop, muse and apply before moving on with Jesus.

The second half of each chapter (The Way of Jesus) is an imaginative meditation on Scripture or tradition. Since several of the Stations are not found in the Gospels and scriptural accounts of the Passion sometimes offer conflicting details, we cannot know for sure how Jesus experienced the Way of the Cross. But that has not prevented people of faith from the fifteenth century (when the devotion was first formalized) to our own day from attempting to reconstruct the events in a prayerful manner.

Epigraphs that precede the Way of Jesus—one from the Hebrew Scriptures, the other from the Christian—may lead the reader into deeper or different meditations on the theme. The Reflection Questions are followed by cruciform Prayers of Action, our guarantee that praying the Way will have political and communal consequences.

My thanks to my editors and friends, Carol Luebering and Lisa Biedenbach, without whose help this book would still be a specter floating in that section of my brain labeled "Good Intentions." My thanks also to those who will cowrite this book by bringing their own experiences of Jesus and his cross to it.

May there be many who find a way that is good for them in these pages. Speaking of prayer, Thomas Merton once observed, "All the old ways are good and all the new ways are good. We can't do everything, so you pick the way that is good for you at the time that is good for you."[3]

[1] Anthony de Mello, *Taking Flight: A Book of Story Meditations* (New York: Doubleday, 1988), p. 27.

[2] Richard Rohr, *Simplicity: The Art of Living*. Translated by Peter Heinegg (New York: Crossroad, 1992), p. 43.

[3] Thomas Merton, *Thomas Merton in Alaska: The Alaskan Conferences, Journals, and Letters* (New York: New Directions, 1988), p. 89.

• I •
STAND FIRM
Jesus Is Condemned

If I will the death of another,
I condemn myself.

OUR WAY

I read about her first in *The New York Times*. My gut reaction
was a disturbing mix of anger, guilt and the admiration I
generally reserve for missionaries in Rwanda or Haiti. Her
name is Sister Helen Prejean. She ministers to murderers and
rapists on death row in the Louisiana State Penitentiary. Her
book *Dead Man Walking* confronts the immorality of the death
penalty in the United States.

As a Sister of St. Joseph of Medaille, Helen Prejean had
committed herself to stand on the side of the poor. She was
working in a housing development when the opportunity to
connect with condemned prisoners opened up before her. She
agreed to be a spiritual adviser to inmate #9528, Elmo Patrick
Sonnier, who, with another man, had murdered two young
lovers.

Sister Helen did not delude herself. Sonnier and the others
she counseled, prayed with and accompanied to the place of
execution were criminals. They were not without sin. But she
insists that "people are more than the worst thing they have
ever done in their life."

By befriending the condemned and being faithful to the
least practiced of the corporal works of mercy, visiting

prisoners, Helen Prejean struck deep to the humanity of each "hardened criminal." They responded, in varying degrees, to her witness as a Christian whose business it was to forgive enemies. They listened when she described the choice that was still open to them: Either die with hearts full of hatred for their "persecutors" (those pushing for the death penalty) or forgive and "die a free and loving man."

Sister Helen has had some forgiving of her own to do. Not everyone applauds her controversial ministry. During the first few years of her death row visits, the nun feared and avoided family members of the victims. Some were vehemently determined that their son's or daughter's death would be avenged; they wanted to see the condemned man "fry." And the Catholics among them did not take kindly to the sister who was showering compassion on the condemned and ignoring them.

When Helen Prejean recognized the pain she had inadvertently caused these families in mourning, she began to meet with their support group, whose motto was "Give sorrow words." She listened to their stories. She learned that they had been victimized two or three times over (first, by the murderer; second, by the criminal justice system; third, by many friends who had abandoned them because these friends could not bear the families' anguish).

The Sister of St. Joseph knew her own insufficiency to ease their sorrow. But she did befriend them—including those who continued to criticize her in public and demonstrate on behalf of the death penalty at every new execution.

In *Dead Man Walking* Helen Prejean writes, "Better, I decide, to try to help ten hurting people—or nine, or one—than to be overwhelmed and withdraw and do nothing—or write an academic paper on The Problem of Evil."[1]

Many in the public, the courts and the prison system oppose Sister Helen; she has been accused of everything from stupidity to indulging in romantic liaisons with the condemned prisoners. Although she has advocated "measured retribution" (nonnegotiable long-term imprisonment) for those who would otherwise be sentenced to death, people say she is "soft on crime" and "a naive little nun."

At first I was angry at Helen Prejean. Angry because she poured the entire alabaster jar of her compassion out on murderers before she commiserated with the parents of their victims. (What if Patrick Sonnier had brutally beaten my son and I read in the paper that some Catholic nun was "coddling the criminal"?) Angry because she was dealing head-on with an issue that made my stomach cringe as though from an overdose of citric acid. (I know the death penalty is wrong. We can't play God. But what is the alternative? I haven't got time to think about it. I can't get involved in another issue.)

Like a gambler who rues the day she made her first trip to Atlantic City, I wish I'd never stepped foot in Sister Helen Prejean's territory. But once read, *Dead Man Walking* clings to your conscience like an unconfessed childhood transgression. I'd like to forget what convicted murderer Robert Lee Willie said to Prejean before he was electrocuted: "Ain't nobody ever called me no son of God before. I've been called a son-of-a-you-know-what lots of times but never no son of God."[2] But I can't. So I pass it on—to prod others to remember.

I remember too what Helen Prejean said early in her ministry when the coals under her feet began to heat up. "I am learning to face things as they come," she said, "not stepping out ahead of grace."[3]

REFLECT

♦ What is my usual gut reaction to people like Helen Prejean who stand firm against injustice in the public forum?

♦ How might her witness change me? Why?

♦ What can we as a faith community do about the death penalty in the United States?

♦

But Moses said to the people, "Do not be afraid, stand firm, and see the deliverance that the LORD will accomplish for you today...." (Exodus 14:13a)

So from that day on they planned to put him to death. (John 11:53)

THE WAY OF JESUS

He looks like a criminal. There's nothing to distinguish him from other Jewish zealots who live on the run.

His face is bruised, his tunic stained like that of a pilgrim of meager substance. His hands are bound as if he had resisted arrest. No advocate has come forward to protest or stand with him before the authorities. Indeed, his friends have either betrayed him, denied him or run away to save their own hides.

The Roman governor, sturdy in the conviction of his power, studies the prisoner. "So," Pilate muses, "this one may provide a diversion." The arrest report reveals that this wandering charismatic Jew actually disarmed his own followers after one had tried to defend him with a sword. The prisoner also claimed to have legions at his disposal, but did not summon them.

"Odd, for one who has aroused so much hatred among these

Sanhedrin fanatics, he hardly looks like someone worth such a
furor," Pilate speculates. "Certainly not a man to be feared. I
find him a curiosity." (The governor had almost said, "an
appealing curiosity." But that would have been going too far.)

Striding toward the prisoner, he watches for a flicker of
submission. When it does not appear, the governor is pleased at
the prospect of a challenge.

"Are you the King of the Jews?" he asks.[4]

Expecting the prisoner to prepare his answer with care,
Pilate is offended by the Jew's immediate response.

"You say so."[5]

The prisoner has confirmed the identity charged against
him. Now the chief priests, provoked by the prisoner's refusal
to be intimidated and fearful that Pilate may not execute their
will, press forward with charges of blasphemy and subversion.
They can still feel the lash of this false Messiah's
condemnation of them in the Temple. He will pay in blood for
disrupting the nation, for defying the Law.

The condemned man says nothing.

"Do you not hear how many accusations they make against
you?"[6] Pilate inquires. Disturbed by the accelerating charges
against his prisoner, the governor sniffs a certain
combustibility in the air. Yet the accused remains silent.

Pilate embraces a new tactic. At the Passover he and his
predecessors have made it their custom to free one prisoner
chosen by the throng of pilgrims gathered at the praetorium. He
will offer these hotheads a real criminal, a proven murderer and
bandit, someone who will make this silent one pale by
comparison.

Relishing the irony of his choice, Pilate presents to the
crowd a notorious prisoner called Jesus Barabbas. Not only
does this swarthy one, wearing the usual sneer of defiance,
share the other prisoner's given name; he is also called

Barabbas, "son of the father" in the language of the streets.

Masking his contempt for the crowd, Pilate displays the two prisoners. He knows that the first had been handed over to him out of fear and envy. The chief priests were threatened by one who worked miracles, preached with authority, consorted with sinners, attracted a considerable following.

"Whom do you want me to release for you, Jesus Barabbas, or Jesus who is called the Messiah?"[7]

While the chief priests and elders are hastily working the crowd, Pilate receives a message from his wife. Calpurnia has had a dream confirming the innocence and righteousness of Jesus. She warns Pilate against participating in this man's death.

The governor has the momentary illusion that he is astride a chasm at a great height. But he takes hold of himself, turning to the crowd once more. They are demanding the release of Barabbas. Pilate is stunned. These deeply religious monotheists display the same cruelty by which he governs.

"Then what shall I do with Jesus who is called the Messiah?"

"Let him be crucified!"

"Why, what evil has he done?"

"Let him be crucified!"[8]

Aware now that the momentum has outstripped him, Pilate decides that his prisoner is not worth a riot on a high holy day. Yet he must dissociate himself from the condemnation of this innocent Jew. His wife's dream implies the possibility of divine retribution, against which Pilate is unarmed.

He acts with expediency. What is needed is a ritual cleansing carried out in plain sight where neither the crowd nor the gods can miss it. He sends for a basin of water and a towel. With pseudo-baptismal gestures writ large, Pilate washes his hands, saying, "I am innocent of this man's blood; see to it yourselves,"[9] he advises them.

The crowd responds without pause or pity: "His blood be on us and on our children!"[10]

Their single-mindedness impresses the governor, who has previously had no qualms about destroying others in pursuit of his own aims.

As is their custom, the Romans will scourge the prisoner before setting him on the road to Calvary.

Meanwhile, outnumbered in the crowd, the friends of Jesus pray silently for the miracle of his release. Surely he has suffered enough and will be spared. Shaken by the horror of the "trial," they hold fast to the memory of his single testimony: He is the Messiah, the deliverer. God's reign of justice and righteousness begins with him. And they must follow.

REFLECT AND INTEGRATE

♦ How does the witness of Jesus in this First Station challenge me?

♦ What does this scriptural scene suggest to me about the role of the believing community in confronting injustice?

♦ How are we as a faith community called to conversion by Pilate and the chief priests?

PRAYER OF ACTION

Jesus,
you
stand
firm
against
the
iron
sway
of unjust power and envious rage.
Your
silence
speaks
to me
of the
condemned
and the
condemner.

In response, I (we) will....

[1] Helen Prejean, C.S.J., *Dead Man Walking: An Eyewitness Account of the Death Penalty in the United States* (New York: Random House, 1993), p. 232.

[2] Ibid., p. 162.

[3] Ibid.

[4] Matthew 27:11b.

[5] Matthew 27:11c.

[6] Matthew 27:13.

[7] Matthew 27:17b.

[8] Matthew 27:22b, 23b, d.

[9] Matthew 27:24b.

[10] Matthew 27:25b.

◆ II ◆
CHOOSE LIFE
Jesus Takes Up His Cross

An unexpected malady
may be
just the thing
the doctor ordered.

OUR WAY

My memory for dates is fading faster than my designer jeans.
But I can cite with certitude the date on which I discovered my
mortality. It was May 27, 1992. I was sitting in a
dermatologist's office, waiting for the white-coated specialist I
had met for the first time that day to give me the results of a
biopsy taken earlier by my doctor in upstate New York.

I was a healthy fifty-three with just a hint of gray and a few
wrinkles that could, I told myself, be taken for laugh lines. My
medical history included basal cell carcinoma. But that breed of
skin cancer does little harm if detected early and promptly
excised. The most recent mole of suspicious nature had been
larger, more amorphous and colorful (bluish-black) than the
previous ones.

Before Dr. Jones removed it from my upper back, he took
Polaroid shots of it and plied me with one-liners like a
wanna-be guest on *Saturday Night Live*. As he worked on the
excision, sweat drenched his face and befogged his glasses. I
was glad it wasn't August.

He told me that the mole might be malignant melanoma. He

17

cheerily added, however, that "it could be a pigmented basal cell carcinoma." I chose the latter possibility. And to show how confident I was in my self-diagnosis, I never even looked up the *M*-words in my skin cancer brochures.

Now the Maine doctor was studying a two-page report with such intensity that I finally faked a cough to remind him that I was still there. He put the papers down, took off his glasses and said in that matter-of-fact tone that is de rigueur at all medical schools, "Mrs. Hutchinson, the biopsy report shows that the tumor Dr. Jones removed was a nodular malignant melanoma, Clark's level four, Breslow's depth 2.375 millimeters."

Echoing his tone, I asked, "What does that mean?" From my perspective of habitual good health, I knew it couldn't mean anything too threatening.

"It means that you have a very serious form of skin cancer that will require immediate attention. We'll call the plastic surgeon today and also put you in touch with an oncologist for a complete screening," he said, rising from his chair.

All his words but one registered in my left brain. If he hadn't said "oncologist," I could have processed the information with the detachment of a research scientist. But that one word clamped itself around my throat, linking me in previously unsuspected ways with extended family members who had died of cancer.

The dermatologist made all the arrangements for me. I drove home in one of those eerie states of consciousness in which we suspect that just over the next hill we may drive right off the edge of the planet, or that the tractor trailer barreling down the opposite lane may hit us head on, and either possibility is quite acceptable because we know there is nothing we can do about it. *Que sera, sera.*

"Yes, indeed, folks. You heard that right. A weird little mole known as malignant melanoma can kill you." I spoke to myself as though I were a TV talk-show host doing an exposé on a mass murderer loose in the land. "That little mole, lurking in perfect, painless silence under your hair, can be the kiss of death. And all it takes is one overdone sunburn in your entire lifetime—especially if you're of Irish descent—to plant this time bomb in your system. Twenty years later it comes back to haunt you like a Dickensian ghost."

Humor helped. But the plastic surgeon would not be able to do the lateral wide excision around the melanoma site for another ten days. That gave my family and friends plenty of time to consider the possibilities. The melanoma might already have slithered its way via the lymphatic system into my brain, liver or lungs. Or it might not. About one-fourth of patients with Clark's level four, stage two-A melanoma do escape without internal complications. I could be one of those. Or I could be one of its victims.

The drag of death is persuasive. After the surgery, I should have been fine. There was no sign the cancer had spread. But I felt vaguely sick every day, tired and heavy like a bear out of hibernation too soon.

I planned my funeral liturgy and grieved nightly in that dark space between wakefulness and blessed sleep. I grieved that my husband might have to live alone in the beautiful house he was building as our sanctuary in the Maine woods. I grieved that I might not be around to see my beautiful granddaughter grow into a graceful and "stately palm tree."[1] I grieved that the beautiful books I had not yet written would, like stillborn infants, wither in the bud. I grieved for my parents, who had counted on me to be the healthy one. (My sister and brother had been diagnosed with multiple sclerosis.)

A small circle of charismatic friends insisted on a healing service, in which they prayed their hearts out over me. I began to climb out of the open grave. Then at a massive healing service conducted by Native Americans at the Tekakwitha Conference in Orono, Maine, a sturdy little woman named Sophie Tellier laid hands on me. When I "woke up," she was bending over me, whispering, "I'm recovering from cancer too." With that, I walked out of the cemetery and vowed to stay out.

I still had to be a periodic regular at the oncologist's office. But now I had the fortitude to choose life. Whatever the melanoma decided to do, it could not stop me from choosing life—and starting every day with an on-my-knees, "Thank you, God, that I am alive and well for another day."

REFLECT

♦ Have I in some way encountered my own mortality? How has that encounter changed me?

♦ Are there ways in which I do not "choose life"? What are they? Why are they?

♦ How are we as a faith community called to minister as healers to those who are sick, or sick of living?

♦

*...I have set before you life and death.... Choose life so that you
and your descendants may live.... (Deuteronomy 30:19b, c)*

*...[W]hoever does not take up the cross and follow me is not
worthy of me. (Matthew 10:38)*

THE WAY OF JESUS

He had made friends with death many times before. Even as a
small child, before he went to the synagogue school, he had
been fascinated by his mother's story of the family's escape
into Egypt. She told him just enough to let him know and
appreciate how Yahweh had spared them from the great sorrow
wreaked by Herod on the little ones of Bethlehem.

With his mother's arms encircling him, Jesus had prayed
with Mary, mouthing phrases of consolation from the Psalms:

...[M]y body...rests secure,
For you do not give me up to Sheol....
...God will ransom my soul from the power of
Sheol,
for he will receive me.
My flesh and my heart may fail,
but God is...my portion forever.[2]

As a youth he had suffered the death of Joseph. He had passed
through the cycle of denial and anger, grieving and healing,
learning to become the man Joseph would have wanted him to
be.

As a man, fresh from the baptismal waters of the Jordan, he
had encountered death in the wilderness—death to the ego's
drive for power and independence from God. Jesus chose life
by rebuking Satan and insisting, "I can live '...by every word
that comes forth from the mouth of God.' "[3]

Later, when his soulmate John the Baptist was slaughtered
in prison, Jesus grieved in a solitary place. Then he chose life

by listening to the distant pleas of the crowd for whom he was moved with pity. He emerged from his retreat to heal the sick and feed the five thousand.

But one encounter comes back to him now most forcibly. It was the day on which his Father had enabled him to break the cords of death that bound his friend Lazarus. He smiled inwardly, remembering how he had progressed from tears and grieving to exultation. "Oh, Lazarus!" he thought, "You were wrapped so tight in burial bands you could hardly move. You couldn't see where you were going. Your legs moved like boards. Yet when they removed the wrappings—I'll never forget the look on your face! You were stunned by the life that was in you. You were radiance itself that day, my friend."

Jesus, his own hands still bound, remembers too the price he paid for Lazarus' radiance. The chief priests and Pharisees had been so threatened by his power that Caiaphas was moved to prophesy: "You do not understand that it is better for you to have one man die for the people than to have the whole nation destroyed."[4] Not wishing to provoke the "prophet" unnecessarily, Jesus had removed himself from public view. He had remained in the dusty town of Ephraim until it was time to prepare for the Passover.

His reverie is short-lived. Pilate's soldiers, who have made perverse sport of him with a brutal crown and a scarlet cloak, are ready to begin the march. They untie his hands. But before he can wipe the blood and sweat from his forehead, a crossbeam is thrust across his shoulders.

Jesus sways under the weight. He has loved wood with his hands, fashioning oak beams and sycamore frames. He has transformed whole trees into smooth boards and decorative spindles. Now he carefully shifts the tree that has been chosen as his companion in death. He refuses to make an enemy of it.

As the macabre procession sets out, Jesus labors to remain

upright and impervious to the jeers of some in the crowd who make him the object of their hatred. There is yet an oasis within, a place where psalms still flourish like date palms.

> My body rests secure,
>> ...you do not give me up to Sheol....
> ...God will ransom my soul from the power of Sheol,
>> ...he will receive me....
> My flesh and my heart may fail,
> but God...is my portion forever.

Jesus moves forward, choosing life with each labored step.

REFLECT AND INTEGRATE

♦ How does the witness of Jesus in this Second Station challenge me?

♦ How has the Church, through its sacramental life, its tradition or its ministers, enabled me to make friends with death?

♦ In what ways might my faith community minister to those who fear death, who are facing death or who are overwhelmed by chronic illness?

♦ How can we as a community give witness that we "choose life"?

PRAYER OF ACTION

Jesus,
Lord of
Life,
Ransomer
from
death,
you bear the cross
unburdened by self-pity, defiance, contempt or
despair.
Help us
choose life,
choose love,
choose
to be
healers.

In response, I (we) will....

[1] Song of Songs 7:7.

[2] Psalms 16:9b-10a; 49:15; 73:26a, c.

[3] Matthew 4:4c.

[4] John 11:50.

·III·
KEEP ON
Jesus Falls the First Time

Even Paul, most sinewy of spiritual athletes, tripped over a hurdle here and there. Shall we require more of ourselves—or others?

OUR WAY

He went to work in the fields at the age of ten, his back bent under the adult yoke of toil and responsibility. The son of migrant workers, born in Yuma, Arizona, César Chavez learned early that living with Lady Poverty was no easy task. He changed schools more often than he did his overalls; high school was a luxury his parents could not give him.

But César was well educated in virtue. His mother taught him to offer hospitality to the hungry—whenever the Chavez family had anything to eat themselves. By their example of perseverance, both parents taught him to keep on despite physical pain, few material rewards and oppression by farmers and growers. In 1939 an adolescent César learned an even more important lesson when his father joined a union for the first time.

Little more than a decade later César became a labor organizer himself among Mexican-American migrants in the Southwest. He registered voters and served as an advocate for those facing deportation. In 1962 he founded the National Farm Workers Association, which later became the United Farm Workers. With his wife Helen and their eight children, he pledged himself to a simple life focused on the nonviolent struggle for justice.

His weapons against growers who used toxic pesticides and treated workers as disposable commodities were daily prayer and Eucharist, fasting, peaceful demonstrations and economic boycotts. Those who opposed him responded with death threats, harassment and character assassination.

After his first major fast in 1968, Chavez observed, "I am convinced that the truest act of courage, the strongest act of humanity is to sacrifice ourselves for others in a totally nonviolent struggle for justice. To be human is to suffer for others. God help us to be human."

In a 1992 interview with peace activist John Dear, S.J., César Chavez affirmed that he still believed in fasting as a primary action against injustice. "Fasting communicates through the soul. I really believe that. I don't know how it happens, but it is the most potent way to communicate that I've ever seen."[1]

Although the UFW made great strides in improving wages and working conditions in the growing fields, the organization suffered many setbacks. Membership fell off; consumers forgot about the grape boycott. Chavez's personal influence waned. His commitment did not.

He was completing a week's fast at the home of a disabled migrant worker when he died of an apparent heart attack on April 23, 1993. Lying beside his body were the court records and union files that symbolized his faithfulness to the cause.

In recent years Chavez had been criticized by many who demand perfection of their heroes. He himself commented, "If the union falls apart when I am gone, I will have been a miserable failure." The nonviolent warrior, Catholic and Christian to the core, had been worn down by life's sorrows. But he was not defeated.

When asked by John Dear what advice he had for other justice seekers, César Chavez replied that nothing less than a lifetime commitment would be acceptable. Responding to Dear's comment, "Like Jesus," Chavez said, "Exactly. He never gave up. He didn't say, 'Well, I'm going to be here just for a little while, and then I'm going to forget you.' He said, 'I'm going to be with you all the time, forever and forever.' "

The boy who bore the yoke at the age of ten had never put it down. Like the Master he followed, César Chavez knew how to keep on.

Let the chant continue: "Viva César Chavez! Viva Jesus Cristo! Viva la Causa!"

REFLECT

♦ To what cause(s) have I made short- or long-term commitments?

♦ How have I formed community with others devoted to these causes?

♦ How have the burdens and falls associated with these causes affected me, my group or community?

♦ How might our faith community integrate the witness of César Chavez?

♦

...[T]hough we stumble, we shall not fall headlong,
   for the LORD holds us by the hand. (Psalm 37:24)

Very truly, I tell you, unless a grain of wheat falls into the earth
and dies, it remains just a single grain; but if it dies, it bears
much fruit. (John 12:24)

THE WAY OF JESUS

Memory was his ally in a throng of adversaries. The grinding
weight of the crossbeam alone might have felled him had he not
retreated in his mind several days to his last procession through
this city that was determined to break his heart. There he was
not burdened but borne on the back of a donkey with fringed
ears and eyes that conveyed an obdurate loyalty.

"Oh, brother ass! How I could use your help. Together we
could bear the tree that now, all unwilling, crushes me," Jesus
thought. His eyes stung as he remembered the beast's kind
eyes. "No one would have to force you to help me. You would
offer your back of your own accord."

His ears recreated the glad shouts he heard then:
   "Hosanna!
   Blessed is the one who comes in the name of the
      Lord—
   the King of Israel!"[2]
The children's voices, wild with the delight of intuitive
recognition, thrilled him: "*Hall lu-yah! Hall lu-yah! Hall
lu-yah, Yesua!*" Leaping back and forth in front of his humble
mount, they had strewn his way with palm branches just as
their ancestors had honored Simon, victorious hero of the
Maccabees, marching into Jerusalem.

Although he had known that many in the crowd praised him
simply because they were swept along in the general exultation,
he had loved the apparent unanimity of it. For once, there

seemed to be no detractors, no holdouts, no hierarchical plotters. He was acclaimed and enveloped in approval. It had been good for him, as wine is good for the reluctant bridegroom.

Distracted by the fire in his shoulders, Jesus stumbles over an errant cobblestone. The crossbeam shifts, creating a forward momentum that he can barely halt by planting both feet like clods that resist the harrow.

He feels unbeaten, able to take whatever the way inflicts. "Great peace have those who love your law;/ nothing can make them stumble."[3] He is not so much praying the psalm as giving himself an exhortation: "No stumbling block, no stumbling block, no block."

Out of the din that accompanies him like the dirge of hired mourners, Jesus catches a few querulous voices. "What a disgrace he is to his mother! What shame she must bear!" a woman exclaims from her window above the street. "Now see what his proud claims have brought him to!" hoots another. "Pity those Galilean fools who threw their lot in with him!"

Smarting under these unexpected lashes, the prisoner loses his concentration. His knees buckle. The tree lurches forward, pinning him to the ground. Warm blood pours from his nose, now disjointed. "Stay back or you'll live to regret it," a soldier threatens. Among the crowd there are those who feast on the pain of others, and they are pressing forward to get their fill.

The prisoner is prodded by the blunt end of a Roman spear. "Get up, Jew! You are not there yet!"

Jesus attempts to obey. But even when the guards lift the crossbeam, he is at first unable to move. Rough hands grab him under the arms, hoisting him to his knees. The stones beneath him are washed in red, and his nose throbs like a drum that is rudely beaten.

"That's enough resting, prisoner. Now on your feet."

He rebels against the weight of so much gratuitous injustice and makes no effort to stand.

REFLECT AND INTEGRATE

♦ How does the witness of Jesus in this Third Station exhort or console me?

♦ What does Jesus' first fall say to me about the call of the believing community in the face of injustice?

♦ What particular injustices in today's world cry out for intercession and advocacy on the part of my faith community?

PRAYER OF ACTION

Jesus,
you
would flee
(if cup
had
passed)
from pack possessed by churlish demons
athirst for another's downfall.
Grant that when the
baying
starts,
we sing
peace
to soothe
the
savage in
every
heart.

In response, I (we) will....

[1] John Dear, S.J., "Cesar Chavez on Voting in the Marketplace," *Pax Christi USA*, Winter (1992), p. 21.

[2] John 12:13b.

[3] Psalm 119:165.

◆IV◆
SHARE THE SORROW
Jesus Meets His Sorrowful Mother

A single look,
a precious word
may prompt
a resurrection.

OUR WAY

Julie was the first of my friends to die. She was six years old and looked like an angel shorn of her locks. The thief that made off with her youth was a rare cancer known as neuroblastoma. Our friendship lasted only a year. But Julie crawled into a cubbyhole somewhere in my psyche, smiling and saying, "Shhh!" Now, whenever she chooses, she emerges to make an unexpected appearance in my prayers or memories or manuscripts.

I wrote about Julie for the first time when she and her mother Doris made a pilgrimage to Lourdes in April 1979. We were among 183 Americans bound from Boston to seek the blue-sashed Lady's intercession. Julie had already borne the rigors of radiation and chemotherapy. But hope bubbled up in her like the waters of Bernadette's spring. Moping was not her style.

Among the mostly adult and teen pilgrims, Julie was the

smallest of all—therefore, the most noticeable. In the dining room, she made the rounds of all the tables like a solicitous maitre d', sampling the guests' meals to assure herself of the menu's quality. (The sampling delighted the guests and satisfied Julie's waning appetite.)

As the pilgrims explored the grotto and its grounds, Doris often found herself pushing an empty wheelchair. Julie had run off to examine a statue of Bernadette or climb up on a rock or greet a tired stranger. Mother and daughter daily lit the tall white tapers symbolizing all pilgrims' reliance on Mary's help. Julie was solemn for these simple rituals.

But at a Palm Sunday liturgy, weighty with vested clergy and wafting incense, she grew restive. Seated down front, close to the ornate altar, she waved to get the attention of her mother, several rows back. Julie then quizzically raised her eyebrows and made a tugging motion toward her synthetic wig. Her coded message was received. With the flourish of a bishop doffing his miter, she removed the offending headpiece and passed it to a young companion as a diversion.

Doris fluctuated between anxiety and trust. "It's hard to say whether I really believed in the beginning that Julie could be cured by a miracle," she later recalled. "But I do know I prayed as hard as I could at the grotto." As Doris and Albert's youngest child and only daughter, Julie was indispensable to their happiness. To consider her death was to confront their own dying.

But after Julie's funeral liturgy on June 17, 1980, Doris found a way to fulfill her daughter's dream and, in doing so, to find a measure of content. Having spent too much of her short life in hospitals or doctors' offices, Julie had decided to be a nurse when she grew up. ("Only I won't give anybody a needle," she confided.)

I recall an incident in a Lourdes hotel room that

foreshadowed Julie and Doris's combined vocation. One evening Julie had a sudden nosebleed which her mother expertly tended while calming the child's fears. The next evening Doris herself suffered a nosebleed and the pilgrimage doctor was sent for. Julie silently observed the doctor's ministrations. Then she began rubbing her mother's back and assuring her that all would be well.

After the doctor left, Julie continued to serve as her mother's bedside nurse. She then turned to me, and in hushed tones so as not to disturb her mother, she said, "Will you watch her for a few minutes? I have to go to the bathroom."

No doubt it was Saint Julie who later interceded for Doris as she hurdled all the economic and academic obstacles to a nursing degree. "Julie had her heart set on being a nurse," Doris observed. "So I became a nurse for her."

Among my photos, cards and drawings from Julie, there is a brilliant magic marker manger scene. There are only two figures in it. One is a blue-robed mother smiling from ear to ear. The other is a purple infant with arms upraised as though asking to be held.

REFLECT

♦ In what meaningful ways have I shared others' sorrows?

♦ How have others in the faith community mothered or fathered me?

♦ What precious words or actions of consolation, like those shared by Doris and Julie, might my faith community offer to those who are sorrowing right now?

♦

Surely he has borne our infirmities
   and carried our diseases.... (Isaiah 53:4a)

Simeon...said to his mother Mary, "This child is destined for
the falling and the rising of many in Israel, and to be a sign that
will be opposed...—and a sword will pierce your own soul
too." (Luke 2:34-35)

THE WAY OF JESUS

They were about to yank the prisoner to his feet when a silent
figure moved purposefully between him and the nearest guard.
Her upper mantle veiled her face and her rough tunic marked
her rural origins. She carried herself with such authority that
the guard stepped back to ease her passage.

Jesus felt her presence before he saw her. It had always
been that way between them. As a small child, he had toddled
after her like a lamb scenting its dam. Her voice was ever music
to him, whether she was lulling or chiding. God had entrusted
Jesus to Mary. The Son, therefore, loved the mother with a
lifelong devotion not accorded in the same way to those who
came later (Magdalene, the Baptist, Peter, John).

How often had he slipped his hand in hers, saying, "Come,
Mother! Come and listen to the turtledoves!" Or, "Come see
how the mustard tree has blossomed" or "Look what father and
I have made!" His enjoyment was not complete until she shared
it.

Even after synagogue school and his apprenticeship in
Joseph's shop divided their daily paths, Jesus and his mother
remained as before, bound by cords of heaven's making. Oh, he
rebelled against her at times; he smiled inwardly to think of it
now. How he had asserted his independence at twelve,
informing his parents that they should have known he had a
higher business to attend to: "Why were you searching for me?

Did you not know that I must be in my Father's house?"[1]

What a look of indignation and loving respect his words had ignited in his mother's face! Both mother and son had resisted the mighty urge to embrace each other, laughing at this new development they welcomed and feared. How glad he was to have had those years after Joseph's death to have been there for her, supporting her less by his trade than by his companionship. Mary had been the envy of those widows whose married sons had little time for them.

His baptism by John had irrevocably altered all his relationships—most especially with Mary. The Father had claimed him in a way no other human ever had or ever would be claimed. After that, God's desire scorched and drove him. "My food is to do the will of him who sent me and to complete his work,"[2] he had told his disciples when they worried about his lack of discretion.

From that point on, only those who gave themselves up to the Father's will as Jesus had could be counted as his kin. He had avoided going out to meet his mother at her request. His refusal and his declaration ("Here are my mother and my brothers!"[3]) tore at her heart like twin vultures.

Jesus had turned his back that day and sought solace by the sea. "Forgive me, Mother," he prayed. "It can be no other way. Each of us must stand on our own two feet and choose. God is all."

At that same hour, on her way home, Mary felt herself strangely mended. She could picture her Son's face without feeling any resentment or pain. "God is all," she prayed.

Now here she was, her dark eyes grown large with grief. He was relieved that she did not weep, did not cry out, did not give in to the horror. Together they entered a silence cleared in the babble of voices around them.

When Jesus had been unable to rise from that first fall, he

had told himself, "Why cooperate so completely with my persecutors? I will drink from the cup my Father has given me. But I will not ease the task of the executioners." He would simply remain there on one knee. It would be up to them to get him and his cross to Golgotha.

No sooner had he made his decision than a voice he vaguely remembered called out within him, "Mother!" It was his own voice, rising up from his childhood, imploring the only one who could save him from bad dreams and treacherous falls to come.

The silence lasted for a few seconds only. But it was time enough for them to tell each other without words that each understood and shared the other's sorrow. Not since he emerged from her womb had they been so united. He saw in her the perfect disciple, the hearth around which his orphaned community could gather in the days ahead.

Just as the guard reached for her arm, Mary firmly touched the upheld face:

—so marred was his appearance, beyond human
semblance,

and his appearance, beyond that of mortals....
(Isaiah 52:14)

Her voice was rich with compassion, projecting the confidence of her Hebrew namesake, who led the women's celebration of victory over Pharaoh's army. And Miriam said, "You are my beloved Son." With that, the guard came between them and she was absorbed into the fluctuating crowd.

The prisoner stood up. He was prepared to go on.

REFLECT AND INTEGRATE

♦ How does the witness of Jesus and Mary in this Fourth Station speak to me?

♦ Who are the cross-bearers we as a faith community are called to uplift and strengthen today?

♦ How do organizations like Amnesty International and Pax Christi serve as channels for the Marian ministry of the Fourth Station? How will we join or support them?

PRAYER OF ACTION

Jesus,
your
sorrow
was
beyond
bearing
until Mary bent her shoulder to halve
the weight of heart and body.
Help us
bend
like
willows
to
touch
the
sorrowed
faces
on our
path.

In response, I (we) will....

[1] Luke 2:49.

[2] John 4:34b.

[3] Matthew 12:49b.

◆ V ◆
STEP FORWARD
Simon Helps Jesus
Carry the Cross

Like a prayer sung,
an unelected
act of service
doubles in value.

OUR WAY

Most of us will put ourselves out to serve another—as long as it is our idea. But let me speak only of my own blindness to the pearls of great price hidden in these "unelected ministries." (We may have here a reverse edification process by which the reader is inspired by how much greater his or her generosity is than the writer's. I once asked a retreat group how many of them had met at least one "unforgivable" person in their lives. I was the only one who raised my hand!)

Years ago, after leaving the monastic life I thought I'd been called to, I was vulnerable as a wolf cub whose mother has been shot. Passing over from a rural cloistered life to a "normal life in the world" was tougher than I had foreseen.

I needed silence; others required stereo or TV companions. I needed solitude; others required conversation about the weather or the daily news. I needed a Spartan environment; others had to have neon and billboards, movies and malls, sales and flea markets.

More than all of that, I needed a way to earn my way back into college while fulfilling—or at least appeasing—those strong spiritual needs. However, I had not yet progressed to job hunting. I told myself that I had to have time to regain my balance and to feel at home in what was once familiar territory.

It was August when Sister Cecilia called. The principal, an industrious Dominican, had pushed herself too hard and suffered a nervous breakdown. She would need a long rest. Her successor would be Sister Mary Mark, teacher of the second-grade boys at our parish school. Would I be interested in taking Mary Mark's place? There were only forty students in the class and I would soon get the hang of it, she cheerily assured me.

How could I tell this woman who had already given thirty years to the service of the Church that I would rather have my toenails pulled out, one by one, without anesthesia, than commit myself to the prison of a parochial classroom? What could I say when she, sensing my instinct to run, added, "Gloria, you are our only hope. We know you can do it"?

"OK, Sister. I'll give it a try."

My gastric juices became as agitated as the witches' brew in *Macbeth*: "Double, double toil and trouble;/Fire burn and cauldron bubble." I was angry, resentful and scared speechless at the prospect of being a substitute teacher for nine penitential months.

"Why did they have to ask me?" I wondered. "They know I'm not a qualified teacher. No doubt they had ten other people turn them down before they got down to asking me. A last resort. A warm body to prop up there in front of forty spitball-making, gum-chewing, teacher-hassling boys who will send me right over the brink."

It took me a few weeks in September to get a grip on reality. The second-graders were normal seven-year-olds with attention

spans of ten minutes, an urgent need to go to the bathroom
frequently and an aptitude for distracting the teacher whenever
she got too wrapped up in her subject.

They made me laugh ("Our Father who aren't in heaven"
and "Forgive us our chest passes"); they made me cry ("Dear
Miss Capone, Billy cannot come to school today because his
grandmother died yesterday. He says his stomach hurts.").
They made me pray ("Lord, I'm so exhausted I can't stand it
and it's only Wednesday. You got me into this. Now keep me
going.").

Their smudged-crayon cards and polished apples assured
me of their affection. And at the end of my nine-month
confinement, I emerged as a strong young adult ready to
immerse myself in the world as I found it rather than as my
romanticized piety would have it.

I had been sure Sister Cecilia chose me because I happened
to be available and couldn't say no. But there may have been
more to it than that.

REFLECT

♦ What "unchosen" ministries have I refused? Which ones
  have I accepted (grudgingly or graciously)?

♦ How have these unsolicited opportunities to serve others
  changed me?

♦ In what ways might your parish or faith community become
  more open to the possibility of "unchosen" ministries? How
  can we as a community remain alert for the times when
  Jesus is about to go by, bearing his cross alone?

♦

For he delivers the needy when they call,
  the poor and those who have no helper. (Psalm 72:12)

As they led him away, they seized a man, Simon of Cyrene, who
was coming from the country, and they laid the cross on him,
and made him carry it behind Jesus. (Luke 23:26)

THE WAY OF JESUS

Jesus walked on in the certainty that his mother and at least a
few of his disciples were walking this bitter path with him. He
knew that neither Magdalene nor John would allow Mary to
come unattended. "They would protect her with their lives, if
need be," he thought.

A proverb bobbed in his mind, distracting him from the
terrible pain in his back and shoulders. "Some friends play at
friendship/ but a true friend sticks closer than one's nearest
kin."[1] How blessed he was to have true friends and true kin!
"For these companions, I thank you, Father. I thank you."

Once again the crossbeam shifted, causing him to cry out
and stumble like one drunk with wine. The captain of the guard
saw that the prisoner might well perish before the sentence was
carried out. "Get a strong back in here at once," he ordered a
subordinate.

Scanning the crowd, the soldier noticed a burly farmer who
stood head and shoulders above the average Jew. His dark skin
shone in the morning sun as he paused to gaze curiously at this
strange procession. "You!" the Roman shouted. "Step
forward!"

Simon's heart lurched as the crowd turned to look at him.
He was a simple man who spent most of his time in the field.
He had never before attracted public attention of any kind. Now
he was under orders to participate in what he realized was an
execution. He cursed his size and the ebony skin that denied

him anonymity. There was no avenue of escape.

"Step forward!" the guard repeated. "You have been chosen to bear the cross of a king. So thank the gods for this great blessing, unworthy one!"

The Cyrenean was unused to sarcasm. But he knew enough not to express any sign of rebellion to a Roman. Instead he looked at the prisoner with an implied accusation. "See what's happening to me because of you? And I don't even know you. I'm an innocent man who deserves better treatment than this. People will take me for a criminal too. What do you have to say to all of this?"

Jesus said nothing as the splintered burden was taken from his own shoulders and laid on Simon's. He understood the Cyrenean's shame and resentment. Yet he did not offer any words of gratitude. He gazed at Simon with love. That was enough.

The gaze startled Simon. At first he took it as an insult. Would this bloodied and obviously despised prisoner dare to look Simon in the face like that if he, the reluctant bearer, were not a North African?

An instant later Simon realized that his gut reaction had deceived him. The prisoner was looking at him as one who knew him well and approved of him without qualification. Without thinking, Simon bowed slightly as Jesus passed in front of him to lead the way.

The cross weighed only half as much on Simon's back. He walked slowly so as not to rush the dying man, who wore a barbarous crown and a tunic drenched in sweat and blood.

"Who is this poor man?" the bearer wondered. "What has he done to deserve such punishment?" Simon felt compassion filling his heart like milk in a pitcher. He was glad that the prisoner had not passed him by.

REFLECT AND INTEGRATE

♦ How does the witness of Jesus and Simon speak to me in this Fifth Station?

♦ A Scandinavian proverb says, "Inside every man there is a king. Speak to the king and he will emerge." ("Inside every woman there is a queen. Speak to the queen and she will emerge.") Who are the royal persons in distressing disguise who need members of my faith community to step forward on their behalf? How might we respond?

PRAYER OF ACTION

Jesus,
no
cross
was
ever
meant
for
one
alone.
You intend us to be bearers
even when we do not choose
the
time
or
place
or
weight or
wood.
So
be it.

In response, I (we) will....

[1] Proverbs 18:24.

♦ VI ♦
BE THERE
Veronica Wipes the Face of Jesus

To have nothing
at hand
to give the hungry
is poverty indeed.

OUR WAY

It was a simple incident. A city dweller might not have
remembered it by the end of the day. The homeless are no more
exotic in Bangor, Maine, than the loggers or farmers from up
north who come in to spend their pay at the mall. We, however,
were woods dwellers temporarily displaced. Like Canada geese
on migration, we were pausing between more secluded sites.

I was on my way out of the shopping center when he caught
my eye. While those who had a choice were arrayed in their
spring plumage, he was swathed in a heavy flannel shirt, wool
pants and a knit cap of indeterminate color. He was standing
alone on a traffic island by the red light, as out of place as a
scraggly spruce in a rose garden. Stoop-shouldered and
untended, he was not without a sense of dignity. Around his
neck hung a sign: "WILL WORK FOR FOOD."

As I approached the light, I noticed that he made no effort
to speak to the occupants of the cars inching their way past him.
His expression made it clear that he was not a beggar. It said,
"I'm not to blame. It could happen to you."

Wedged in by cars fore and aft, I ransacked my purse for

whatever cash might be mixed in with grocery coupons and old shopping lists. My blind fingers found no currency of any kind, only useless change. "Why did I switch to direct deposit?" I upbraided myself, feeling like a traitor for my middle-class reliance on checks and plastic.

My face reddened as I moved up in line. "My God, he sees me!" I thought. "He sees me in this big car passing him by. If he curses me, I won't feel any worse than I do already." Having imaged myself as the Samaritan, I was forced to play the Levite.

The signed man neither cursed or scowled. He simply observed as each rescue ship sailed on by. The sour taste of shame for our collective insularity against his need made me fumble for the Rolaids.

"Don't go away. I'll be back."

Whether the man received my telepathic message, I could not be sure. Whenever the traffic opened up, I ignored the speed limit signs and made it back to our apartment in record time. Reason cautioned me to take care of the groceries first (ice cream melting in the trunk, vegetables wilting), but for once I told reason to take a hike.

Like a kid on an Easter egg hunt, I scurried through the apartment, searching every possible hiding place for money "put aside." When I came up with two tens and a five, it was alleluia time. I rushed back to the shopping center, repeating a mantra: "Be there. Be there. Be there."

He had not retreated from the midday heat. He stood exactly as he had before, undaunted by the procession of drivers who looked past him at more interesting diversions. I pulled out of the offending stream of traffic and swung around behind the island.

Eager to assuage his failure, I walked quickly toward him. He turned with a guarded look. His face was badly sunburned, his neck scrawny in someone else's collar. He was careful to expect no more than he had already received. I might be a tourist asking directions or a self-righteous rebuker of the indolent. I smiled.

"I'm sorry I don't have any work for you," I said. "We live in one of those apartment complexes where everything is taken care of. But please take this."

He looked relieved and raised his hand slowly, as though his arm might have fallen asleep during the long vigil. I placed the folded bills in his palm. "It isn't much," I said, only dimly aware of how true that was.

He glanced down, assured himself it was indeed cash in his hand. Without unfolding it or showing undue curiosity, he doffed his oil-stained cap and replied, "Thank you. I'll pay you back." "No, no. There's no need." Instantly I realized my mistake. I should have said, "OK, but there's no rush" or anything that would have acknowledged our equality. I remembered having to accept money from a friend in a crisis. When I kept worrying about how and when I could repay her, she observed, "Don't you know it's more blessed to receive than to give?"

Standing there with the homeless man I knew it full well. However he arrived at this state and whatever use he was about to make of those folded bills was not mine to judge. In his poverty, he forgave me for playing the well-heeled philanthropist. He gave me a smile and said, "Have a nice day." It felt like a blessing. His "WILL WORK FOR FOOD" sign was slightly askew and his missing teeth gave him a comical appearance.

"Thanks. I will," I promised, sure that I had just encountered a holy fool.

REFLECT

♦ What is my usual response when I encounter a homeless person, a panhandler or some other social outcast in a public place?

♦ How have I enabled or allowed those in need to give back to me? How have these encounters changed me?

♦ In what ways might your faith community advocate change in an economic system that divides us into beggars, donors and blind passers-by?

♦

Give liberally and be ungrudging when you do so, for on this account the LORD your God will bless you in all your work and in all that you undertake. (Deuteronomy 15:10)

Whoever welcomes a prophet in the name of a prophet will receive a prophet's reward; and whoever receives a righteous person in the name of a righteous person will receive the reward of the righteous. (Matthew 10:41)

THE WAY OF JESUS

The prisoner straightened up, surprised at how little solidity his body had without its attendant burden. He was lightheaded from hunger and dizzy as a child who has spun himself like a top. The sound of Simon's footsteps echoing his own consoled him. David's song gave him fresh courage: "Though an army encamp against me,/ my heart shall not fear."[1]

Jesus had no idea how derelict he appeared. His cheeks were bruised from the blows of the soldiers who had mocked him as a false prophet. His nose was broken, his beard matted with blood. The grotesque crown of thorns gave him the look of a possessed man playing the fool. Many in the crowd turned their heads slightly to avoid the full disclosure of his face. Others masked themselves in contempt as though to ask, "What have we to do with the likes of you?"

Among the onlookers was a woman named Veronica. Out of curiosity and boredom, she had once gone to hear the strange rabbi from Nazareth preach from a hillside in Capernaum. And what a preacher he was! His voice rang like a bell of warning; his eyes burned with the fire of righteousness. He strode up and down, confronting first this group and then that. His words alternately stung like a father's correction and inspired with a mother's trust.

Many that day in Capernaum had been branded by his teaching. They no longer belonged to themselves but to Jesus of Nazareth, a prophet and possibly more. Recalling her own inclination to be swept away at the time, Veronica told herself, "How right I was to avoid taking up with his followers! They too will be in jeopardy now. I have enough troubles of my own without having to worry about Roman dogs yapping at my heels."

As the prisoner approached, Veronica recalled one of the Beatitudes he had proclaimed to the crowd on the hillside: "Blessed are those who are persecuted for righteousness' sake, for theirs is the kingdom of heaven."[2]

"Today you personify this Beatitude, Rabbi," she thought. "No one can accuse you of preaching God's justice while protecting your own hide."

As Jesus passed directly in front of her, Veronica gasped involuntarily. "Poor man, what have they done to you? What have they done?"

The contrast between his poverty and dereliction and her own privileged state struck the woman like a husband's blow.

Her head ached with consternation. "Look at him! And no one's lifting a finger to help him. What's the matter with these people? I'm not even one of his disciples and I can't stand to see such suffering."

She had to do something. He would soon be out of sight, cut off from her by the gawkers and the guards. She clutched her upper mantle closer to her face and began elbowing her way towards the prisoner. She had no idea what she would do if she reached him. A few male onlookers were already giving her suspicious glances to which she responded with a defiant stare.

Now only one Roman stood between Veronica and her goal.

As she caught his eye, she quickly removed her veil as though she were a prostitute or one of the lowborn. Surprised by this sudden display of Hebrew beauty in a public place, the guard allowed her to pass.

Veronica dropped to her knees in front of the prisoner, who leaned toward her. In the moment that was given, she held her veil to his face, cleansing it as a mother ministers to her hurt child.

"You shall have your reward, daughter," he said with a smile that looked bizarre on such a tortured face.

"No, Teacher, I deserve none. Forgive me for not coming to you sooner," she replied, as the guard lifted her out of the way, saying, "Don't try my patience, woman."

Aware now of the barrage of insults aimed at her for appearing bareheaded, Veronica once again donned the veil that had caressed the Teacher's face. This time she had not refused his offer of discipleship.

REFLECT AND INTEGRATE

♦ How does the witness of Jesus and Veronica speak to me in this Sixth Station?

♦ As Job had his three comforters, so Jesus had Mary, Simon and Veronica on the way to Calvary. Job's comforters proved themselves false by insisting on his guilt in order to explain his suffering. In what ways are Mary, Simon and Veronica true comforters?

♦ How might our faith community emulate Jesus' comforters in ministry to those who are rejected in their suffering (AIDS patients, panhandlers, the mentally disturbed, prisoners, drug addicts, the elderly poor)?

PRAYER OF ACTION

Jesus,
we
long
to
see
your
holy
face.
Yet our eyes glaze over with rejection
when the burned and hollowed faces
of beggars heave into view.
Remove
the
veil
of
our
defenses
that
we
may
earn
love's
reward.

In response, I (we) will....

[1] Psalm 27:3a.

[2] Matthew 5:10.

◆ VII ◆
UPLIFT THE BROKEN
Jesus Falls the Second Time

When the girl fell off the flying rings, her gym instructor said, "Grab those rings again right now or you'll never get past the fear."

OUR WAY

We are waiting in the main lobby. An inattentive visitor might think he'd wandered into a nice middle-class hotel rather than a hospital. There are tasteful paintings (including a portrait of Lincoln looking burdened at his desk) and flowers, chairs that comfort, TVs set in alcoves and kept at an unobtrusive volume, an air of gracious ease. Yet behind their newspapers and idle glances, the occupants are charged with tension.

At intervals a volunteer at the main desk speaks into her microphone: "Will a member of the O'Malley family please come to the registration desk?" One or two people rise and walk toward the desk like defendants approaching the bench. They are instructed to pick up a phone. A voice from the operating room assures them that the surgery is over. Their loved one is sleeping it off in the recovery room.

Two hours have passed since my mother's surgery began: a simple gallbladder removal. Farewell to the wrenching pain in her back and the intestinal difficulties. Home in a day or two. A doctor in his O.R. greens, mask hanging loosely around his neck like an off-duty outlaw, unexpectedly appears in the lobby. The hotel image is blown away by his presence.

We will not have to go to the desk, pick up the phone and listen to a disembodied voice. Dr. B. is here to tell us that the gallbladder was not the culprit after all. (Dear God, here comes the *C*-word again!) Cancer in the liver, the pancreas, maybe other sites unknown. "It doesn't look too good," says Dr. B., standing close to us to lend support. (How many times has he had to be the messenger who brings sad tidings and announces dire prognoses?)

My father seems to be anesthetized; comprehension will come later. "Come on, Pop. We'll go home for a while," my husband tells him. "Mom will be in the recovery room for another hour or so." Pop thinks that's a good idea. Somewhere beyond the sliding glass doors of the lobby, normalcy can still be found. He needs a strong dose of it to steady the rocking world.

I find a chair by the desk marked "Chaplain." She is making her rounds, anointing the patients with prayer and optimism. They need her more than I do. I can just sit here out of the way and cry for my mother, cry for the seventy-nine years that have passed without allowing her enough time to esteem her own gifts, cry for the loss of solitude she must need but never has, cry for the childhood memories of not quite meeting her mother's expectations, cry for a life too much consumed by doing for others what they might have done for themselves.

Now I am falling apart in the ladies' room, flushing toilets and running water in the sinks to muffle sobs that might "unman" others who have better contained their sorrow. "Go do something for Mom. You'll feel better." The inner voice makes sense. Take refuge in action.

In the hospital gift shop, I find a mauve ceramic angel, head cupped in its hands and bent forward as though engaging its

owner in conversation or communal silence. Had I seen it at
any other time, I might have judged it pathetic. Today I need to
believe in this symbol of guardianship.

The volunteer behind the counter greets me, looks again and
becomes a hovering pelican. Such an angel must have a box, he
says, rushing off to get just the right one. He makes small talk
to bury sorrow. Feigning a lack of expertise, he engages me in
wrapping the gift. One by one he passes me strips of Scotch
tape, holds his thumb on the ribbon so it can be properly tied,
hands me the scissors for curling. I laugh inwardly at the
analogy between him and an O.R. nurse assisting at a mundane
surgery.

He stands back to admire our handiwork. "There. That
should do it!" he says, smiling hope in my direction. Then he
turns to attend to customers whose needs he has assessed as less
immediate.

With the simplest acts of kindness, that discerning
volunteer has helped me to get back on my feet. The angel and
I will be prepared to greet my mother when she wakens.

REFLECT

♦ Who or what has helped me to get up after I have fallen into
   depression or hopelessness?

♦ In what ways have I done the same for others?

♦ How might our faith community minister to the families of
   the sick and dying, to those who feel broken by life, who
   suffer from depression or who are overwhelmed by their
   inability to cope with everything that must be done for one
   who is terminally ill?

Give light to my eyes, or I will sleep the sleep of death,
and my enemy will say, "I have prevailed." (Psalm 13:3b-4a)

Now to him who is able to keep you from falling, and to make
you stand without blemish in the presence of his glory with
rejoicing...be glory...now and forever. (Jude 1:24, 25b, d)

THE WAY OF JESUS

He has drawn strength from his comforters and they have
sustained him. Simon is still bearing the cross behind him. The
prisoner scans the crowd on either side, hoping to absorb the
empathy of others who are with him in his deprivation. No face
welcomes him; no word of comfort reaches him from the oasis
of the uncondemned.

Jesus is once again in the garden among the mute olive
trees. "I am deeply grieved, even to death," he had said to Peter,
James and John; "remain here, and stay awake with me."[1] He
had stripped himself, letting his great need appear naked before
them. Certain of their compliance, he had gone apart from them
a little and pressed himself to the earth in prayer.

He had begged his Father to let the cup pass him by; yet he
had also accepted the destiny of expiation for all who, in the
inconstant humanity which he understood so well, had turned
and would turn against the Father. Jesus had summoned the
strength to do it because he knew he was not alone. The Father
was with him. His intimate companions were with him.

Even now his heart bolted against the heavy reality of their
weakness. He could not believe it when he found them with
their heads hidden in their cloaks, their eyes closed to his
tribulation. He had roughly shaken Peter, whose failure cut him
deepest. "So could you not stay awake with me one hour?" he
had asked incredulously. "Stay awake and pray that you may
not come into the time of trial."[2]

Oh, they meant well. They intended to be there for him. But their flesh recoiled from contact with the unnamed beast aprowl in the night garden. The sharing at the Passover supper had pushed them beyond their emotional limits. Their liberation songs had never been sung with more fervor. Yet once they had eaten the bread that was his body and drunk the wine that was his blood, their hearts were constrained in the fowler's snare.

He was everything to them. They simply could not bear the reality of his impending death.

So when he said, "Keep watch with me," they retreated. The fruit of the vine, imbibed earlier from several blessing cups, came to their aid. They would sleep and know nothing. They would sleep and the horror would creep away into some other Gethsemane, some other time. They would sleep until they could wake up to a bearable reality. Jesus, their Rock, would be there. Nothing could harm him, or them. The enemy would not prevail against the shepherd or his flock.

"Oh, Peter, where are you now? Where are you when I need to see your stalwart face?"

His friend's betrayal strikes him anew. In that instant, his strength deserts him and he falls. The stones become his bed. He does not want to rise. Surely he has come far enough. Rest is what he needs now. Rest.

"This is my beloved Son. On him my favor rests."

The voice that is as much his own as the one with which he spoke to his disciples rouses him. It lifts him, setting him back on his feet, firm on his way.

Jesus walks on, bearing on his own back all those whom the beast stalks.

REFLECT AND INTEGRATE

♦ How does the witness of Jesus uplift you in this Seventh Station?

♦ In what ways do you identify with the three friends in the garden?

♦ In its worship, reflection on the word of God and ministry, how might your faith community be called to recognize and respond to the wish for death or oblivion that comes to most of us at one time or another? How might these experiences strengthen gratitude for life—in ourselves and others?

PRAYER OF ACTION

Jesus,
your
friends
sought
refuge
in
the
small
death
of
sleep.
Give light to our eyes when it is time to keep
vigil against the beast that purrs surrender.
Light
your
glory
lamps
in us
that
we may
lift
up
the
fallen.

In response, I (we) will....

[1] Matthew 26:38.

[2] Matthew 26:40b-41a.

THE PLATEAU
We Will Walk With Each Other

The first seven Stations are behind us. We have seen clearly that the Way of Jesus is not a solitary way. He seeks and receives comfort, human and divine. Our lives mirror this need for solidarity.

When Father Jerzy Popieluszko became a political activist on behalf of Polish shipyard workers, he relied on the support of the workers' families and absorbed strength from the massive congregations that gathered for his monthly "Mass for the fatherland." His bold public outcry against the government and the secret police was enabled by God's grace and the people's ministry to him. Before he was martyred in 1984, Popieluszko had already achieved the freedom of a saint who can say, "The source of our captivity lies in the fact that we allow lies to reign, that we do not denounce them, that we do not protest against their existence every day of our lives."

Like the Mother of Jesus on the Way of the Cross, Jerzy Popieluszko was not deterred by the flashing of swords, the trampling of military feet or the rending of hierarchical garments. Each was there for Jesus.

When Elba and Celina Ramos went to work as housekeepers for the Jesuits at the University of Central America in San Salvador, they had no idea how much their ministry would cost them. By publicly aligning their lives with those of the justice-seeking priests, the two women agreed to walk under the shadow of the cross.

Like Simon of Cyrene, Elba and Celina agreed to share

Christ's burden. The priests they served were considered "outlaws" by those who would not allow progressive social change in El Salvador. The assassins of November 1989 did not differentiate. They killed the two women along with the six Jesuits. Elba and Celina, Ignacio Ellacuría, Segundo Montes, Ignacio Martin-Baró, Amando López, Juan Ramón Moreno and Joaquin López y López—each was there for Jesus.

When Kathryn McCabe saw a three-year-old Bosnian undergoing surgery to remove shrapnel without benefit of anesthesia, the American homemaker wept. She thought of her own four healthy and secure children. And she wondered why someone wasn't smuggling medical supplies into war-torn Bosnia.

Unable to find anyone who would do what needed to be done, Kathryn McCabe of Sylvania, Georgia, organized a group of mothers. She called them "Mary's Hands." Like Veronica on the road to Calvary, they stepped in to tend the bleeding Christ. They willingly placed themselves in danger in order to deliver medical supplies for women and children in Bosnia. Each was there for Jesus.

As we move on to the final seven Stations, we link arms with all the frontline justice, peace and compassion people of Poland and Bosnia, Central and South America, the Middle East and our own afflicted country. We link arms in order to be empowered by their witness and to amplify its effect.

Together we learn and learn again that we are dependent on the God who sees Jesus through his passion and up out of the abyss. Our voices too are joined in battle cry:

For I know that my Redeemer lives,
  and that at the last he will stand upon the earth;
...whom I shall see on my side,
  and my eyes shall behold, and not another. (Job 19:25, 27)

✦ VIII ✦
CRY JUSTICE!
Jesus Meets the Women

To hold your tongue
in the presence of injustice
may save your hide
but mortally wound
your soul.

OUR WAY

When the institutional Church fails to practice the justice it so
movingly proclaims to the world, we are all diminished as
Catholics. Likewise, when any one of our members looks
straight at injustice and says, "This act defiles the Reign of
God. I will stand against it," we are all enriched.

How each of us chooses to stand and cry "Justice!" is a
matter of call, conscience and opportunity. Some organize
politically; others gather gospels in hand and ask, "What does
Christ require of us in this situation?" Some demonstrate in the
streets; others infiltrate immoral institutions, working change
slowly from within. Some protest in righteous anger; others
weep repentance for the "dead and dry."

What beautiful earthen vessels adorn our house! Their
presence does us proud and prods us to the purpose for which
we were baptized. Look closely. Pray the following litany.

American Archbishop Rembert Weakland, preaching
pacifism and "the preferential option for the poor," wonders

how Catholics can hear the word of God proclaimed Mass after Mass and "go home and feel comfortable." Pray for us, all preachers of justice!

Joan Chittister, O.S.B., teaching "patient endurance" and steadfast resistance against sexism, militarism and economic injustice, urges us not to lose our souls in anger or frustration to those who perpetuate violence. Pray for us, all teachers of justice!

Penny Lernoux, writing as a journalist in Latin America, exposed the complicity of the United States government in human rights violations against the poor and challenged us to a political activism committed to gospel values. (Lernoux, author of *Cry of the People*, worked without respite on behalf of the poor. She died of cancer on October 8, 1989.) Pray for us, all doers of justice!

Arturo Rodriguez, together with Helen Chavez, widow of César, organizes a three-hundred-mile pilgrimage through the San Joaquin Valley and calls us to join forces with those who will not abide agribusiness abuse of farmworkers. Pray for us, all you poor who carry the flag of justice!

Joanne Navarre, teacher and catechist in the Lafayette, Louisiana, diocese, creates a program called Effective Black Parenting to inculcate pride in African-American heritage as well as family and spiritual values. She summons us to the rescue of neglected children and youth who are spinning, rudderless, in an impassive sea. Pray for us, all you champions of Christ's forgotten children!

Birgil Kills Straight, an Oglala Lakota, together with other Native American activists like Maria Braveheart Jordan, a Hunkpapa Lakota, petition the pope to revoke an ancient papal bull that has been used to help justify the seizure of indigenous lands. They urge us to educate ourselves on how the Church and the government must cooperate in returning and preserving

Native Americans' sacred lands. Pray for us, all you warriors of justice!

For all the ways we have been vessels of your justice, Lord, we thank you.

For all the ways we have neglected to be the person who does justice, we weep repentance.

REFLECT

♦ In what ways have I suffered from injustice—in the Church or in the world?

♦ Who or what has prodded and enabled me to be a person who does justice?

♦ How can my faith community or my family respond to the above litany?

♦

By the rivers of Babylon—
there we sat down and there we wept
when we remembered Zion. (Psalm 137:1)

The twelve were with him, as well as some women who had
been cured of evil spirits and infirmities: Mary, called
Magdalene, and Joanna, ...and Suzanna, and many others, who
provided for them out of their resources. (Luke 8:1c-2, 3b)

THE WAY OF JESUS

Their keening pierces his pain like a marksman's arrow. The prisoner lifts his head. He has been focusing on his feet, willing the left to follow the right, watching their labored progress with detachment. He has blocked out the mindless jibes of onlookers and the complaints of his uniformed escort.

The weeping women of Jerusalem stand as witnesses to the enormity of that injustice by which innocence is condemned, the Savior is slain, the Word silenced. The children, clinging to their mothers' knees or sucking their thumbs for security, whimper without comprehending the terror that has been set loose.

He was known as a friend of women and children—a reputation his male disciples had at times tried to refute. They thought it unseemly that he should publicly defend a prostitute, allow himself to be touched by a hemorrhaging woman, theologize with a Samaritan woman of dubious character and dandle babies on his knee when there was work to be done.

Jesus loved the company of women, recognizing them, regardless of their wealth or status, as among the *anawim* (God's poor) of their time and place. Often when he felt in need of some pleasant reward, he would find a pretext to appear at the door of Martha and Mary in Bethany. He was as much at home there as in his mother's house. And he never denied, to himself or to them, the appeal of their physical grace, their voices warm as bread, their receptivity to him.

"Daughters of Jerusalem," he says to them, "do not weep for me; but weep for yourselves and for your children."[1]

As he speaks, he is remembering his own tears over Jerusalem as he foresaw continued rejection by his own people. How he loved the Jews of Jerusalem! And how they resisted him, defending themselves against a vulnerable Messiah.

The women have stopped wailing. Like deer sensing distant smoke, they stand alert, waiting and wary. Why must they weep for themselves, for their children? What is the Teacher trying to tell them as he approaches his own death?

"For the days are surely coming when they will say,

'Blessed are the barren, and the wombs that never bore, and the breasts that never nursed,'" he responds. "Then they will begin to say to the mountains, 'Fall on us'; and to the hills, 'Cover us.' For if they do this when the wood is green, what will happen when it is dry?"[2]

It is a prophet's warning. When the Jews rise up against the Romans, the Empire will have its revenge. The Temple will be destroyed, the Jews scattered like hapless sheep. They will long for death but endure a bitter exile. Their tears shall be rivers of remembrance for Zion.

Like Jesus himself, the women and their children and grandchildren are grain to be ground by the millstone of injustice. The powers and principalities will one day be vanquished. But in the interim, there is solace in mutual love and steadfast moral resistance.

They reach out to him as he passes.

REFLECT AND INTEGRATE

◆ How does the witness of Jesus and the women call me out of myself?

◆ In what ways have I been or will I be a friend of the women who suffer injustices in society and in the Church?

◆ How do we want our faith community to "cry justice"?

PRAYER OF ACTION

Jesus,
you
were
riven
by
rejection,
wounded
by the
unjust.
Yet you were comforted by the company of women
whom you called to vigilance for justice.
Alert
us,
the "fit-
for-
burning,"
to do
justice
while
we can.

In response, I (we) will....

[1] Luke 23:28.

[2] Luke 23:29-31.

◆ IX ◆
CRY COMPASSION!
Jesus Falls the Third Time

Full-bosomed mercy
always comes as a surprise,
like arms wrapping us round
when we feel least lovable.

OUR WAY

Thomas Merton, Trappist hermit and renowned spiritual writer, was a man of many successes (which he denigrated but sometimes openly courted) and multiple sorrows. Prayer was his life. Wisdom was his quest. God, above all, was his love. Often at cross purposes with his religious superiors and critics of his peace and social justice stances, he suffered the consequences of trying to live truthfully.

At fifty-three Merton was given permission to travel to Asia for an East-West conference on monasticism. Years of contemplation and ongoing conversion had made him familiar with that mysterious being known as the "true self." So when he set out for Asia, Merton intuited that he was "going home" to a place whose threshold he had never before crossed. (Having lost both parents when he was young and lived in more places than he could count, Merton had a deep need to be "at home.")

Merton believed that he would find what he sought. That conviction had been reinforced year after year as he, like Jonah rocking in the belly of the whale, entrusted his destiny to God. Merton, the spiritual orphan who had tasted life's bitterest fruit, gave his life to God and said, metaphorically, "Take the helm. Where You sail, I will follow."

And God responded: "I have always overshadowed Jonas with my mercy, and cruelty I know not at all. Have you had sight of me, Jonas, my child? Mercy within mercy, within mercy."[1]

Evidence of God's overshadowing is evident in every book Merton wrote—and in much written about him after his death. From his unlikely best-seller *The Seven Storey Mountain* (1948) to the most recent collections of his private correspondence, we see him tripping, falling and falling again. (Isn't it his unfailing honesty about his own weakness and blindness—which we recognize as our weakness and blindness—that endears him so much to us?)

Before his conversion, he falls into skepticism and atheism. Mercy lifts him up.

He tumbles into sexual excess and drunkenness. Mercy lifts him up.

After his conversion, he trips over his conflicting desires for solitude and sociability, for anonymity and fame. Mercy lifts him up.

He falls in love with a young nurse and nurtures illusions of "spiritual marriage." His vows of celibacy and stability wobble like cracked pillars in a sagging temple. Yet Mercy lifts him up.

Mercy set Thomas Merton down in Asia where he journeyed from India to Tibet to Ceylon to Bangkok. And there among the great-souled spiritual masters of the East, America's best-beloved monk found what he was looking for.

At Polonnaruwa in Ceylon, Merton reverently approaches the giant Buddhas carved into the landscape. He takes off his shoes, aware that he is on holy ground. He is cradled in silence, wooed by the tranquil smiles of the great stone figures. They overpower him with their clarity and serenity. They speak of that reality which is right in front of us yet unseen.

Later he attempts to describe the experience. Those of us who have not consorted so habitually with wisdom hear his voice as from a great distance. "All problems are resolved and everything is clear, simply because what matters is clear. The rock, all matter, all life is charged with *dharmakaya* [a Sanskrit term for "the essence of all beings"] ...everything is emptiness and everything is compassion."[2]

On December 10, 1968, in Bangkok, Thomas Merton delivered a talk on "Marxism and Monastic Perspectives." In it he spoke of that spiritual liberty that "nobody can touch" and no circumstances can destroy. Informing his audience that he would respond to questions after the lunch break, he lightly remarked, "So I will disappear."

After lunch Merton took a shower. No doubt he was anticipating the afternoon's dialogue with his brother and sister monastics when he was accidentally electrocuted by a faulty electric fan.

By his life of prayer ("How I pray, is breathe," he once observed),[3] by his fidelity to solitude ("It is not a question of my choosing solitude; it is she who has chosen me"[4]), and by his fidelity in love ("Remembering that I have been a sinner, I will love You in spite of what I have been, knowing that my love is precious because it is Yours"[5]), Merton was prepared to see.

What he saw was that "everything is compassion."

No matter how often we fall or how far out of control we spin, the center holds. We are held and overshadowed. We are wound, as poet Gerard Manley Hopkins wrote, "With mercy round and round...."[6]

REFLECT

♦ What memorable encounters with the sacred (or what meaningful religious experiences) have I had?

♦ How have I experienced God's mercy and compassion?

♦ How might my faith community embody God's maternal "mercy within mercy" for those who have fallen into sin or addiction?

♦

Many are the torments of the wicked:
but steadfast love surrounds those who trust in the LORD.
(Psalm 32:10)

But while [the Prodigal Son] was still far off, his father saw
him and was filled with compassion; he ran and put his arms
around him and kissed him. (Luke 15:20)

THE WAY OF JESUS

Without turning to look, he knows that the women and children are following after him. Their vigilance is sharpened by the sight of him. The green wood goes before the dry. Simon's pace slackens in sympathy with the prisoner. But a guard soon prods him on.

As Jesus attempts to press on, lest the Cyrenean bear the escort's wrath, he falls without warning like a slender yew before the axe. Stretched full length upon the ground, he dreams that he is sinking deep into the womb of the earth, a sweet, dark and watery haven. He is as safe here as he was in Egypt, far from Herod's bloodied swords.

"*Abba*," he prays. "Are you here? Are you with me?"

Jesus rests in the silence, waiting for an answer.

He sees himself surrounded by a large crowd. Among them are tax collectors and prostitutes, usurers and beggars, adulterers and abusers. They are looking to him for a lift up out of the mire. Keeping their distance are scribes and Pharisees, who berate him for his fellowship with sinners.

He tells them a story about a father who has two sons. The elder son, like a good Pharisee, knew and obeyed the Law with a careful rectitude. He loved his father and felt sure that he, in turn, had earned his father's love.

The younger son was a creature of contradictions. He too loved his father. But he yearned for experiences that might appease the appetites of his unruly body, mind and spirit. So he insisted on having the whole of his inheritance that he might go off and seek fulfillment. He scarcely noticed how ineptly he had broken his father's heart.

During his absence, the younger son fell repeatedly into the snares of wrongheadedness. He spent himself and his resources. Hired to feed a farmer's swine, the lost son found himself fallen so low that he now envied these indolent pigs for the pods they mindlessly devoured.

Mercy lifted the young man by the elbow and said, "Go home to your father. Own up to your sin and stupidity. Say 'I no longer am worthy to be called your son.' "

And when the prodigal came into view, his father raced down the hill, endangering life and limb, bursting with a compassion that knew no bounds. And the father threw his arms around the son, kissing him first on one cheek and then the other, dancing with elation and crying, "My son, my son!"

Jesus hears the Father's voice. He knows that if the lost son is lifted up, the innocent Son is surely encompassed by Mercy. "I entrust myself to you, Father," he says aloud. "I entrust myself to you."

The sound of his own voice breaches the womb. He is pulled from the earth by those who obey Caesar's law and remain illiterate in the tongue of conscience.

They are approaching the holy ground where Jesus will reveal to all who seek enlightenment that "everything is compassion."

REFLECT AND INTEGRATE

♦ Do I really believe that I am always encompassed by Mercy? Why or why not?

♦ Who are the people in my life who may need me to emulate the compassionate father?

♦ What might we as a family or community do to help others trust in the reality of God's mercy?

PRAYER OF ACTION

Jesus,
three
times
felled,
yet
not
defeated,
call us home from our wandering,
raise us up from the earth.
Empty
us
of
all
that
displaces
mercy
and
compassion.

In response, I (we) will....

[1] Thomas Merton, *The Sign of Jonas* (New York: Doubleday, 1956), pp. 351-52.

[2] James Finley, *Merton's Palace of Nowhere: A Search for God through Awareness of the True Self* (Notre Dame, Ind.: Ave Maria Press, 1978), p. 108.

[3] Thomas Merton, *The Courage for Truth: Letters to Writers. Selected and edited by Christine M. Bochen* (New York: Farrar Straus and Giroux, 1993), p. 28.

[4] Thomas Merton, *The Asian Journal* (New York: New Directions, 1973), p. 235.

[5] Thomas Merton, *Thoughts in Solitude* (New York: Farrar Straus Giroux, 1958), p. 100.

[6] "The Blessed Virgin Compared to the Air We Breathe," *The Poems of Gerard Manley Hopkins*, ed. W. H. Gardner and N. H. MacKenzie (London, New York: Oxford University Press, 1967).

CRY HUMANITY!
Jesus Is Stripped

To prove their mettle
against the armored Romans,
ancient Celtic warriors
rushed naked into battle.
By sheer force of will,
they turned vulnerability
into power.

OUR WAY

I have never been stripped by prison guards or customs officers. But the blush that covers me at the thought of it engenders a powerful empathy for those who have been. Most of us have merely been singed by the brush fire of bodily humiliation. We may have endured it in a doctor's office, a hospital ward or a nursing home.

Clothing is our fragile barrier against invasion; it is the camouflage by which we evade detection. When I am undressed in the presence of one not bonded to me by love, I am, in some sense, at their mercy. If a nurse is brusque with her "Take off your clothes" or a physician opens my "johnny" as though he's flipping a page in *Sports Illustrated*, I feel violated. If my body is a temple, it should not be treated as an objectified sight in someone else's tourist guidebook.

What I can only guess at, Sheila Cassidy knows firsthand. While serving as a physician in Chile during a time of upheaval, she was arrested for providing medical care to "revolutionaries." Her captors would have released her had she divulged the names of others in the resistance. She refused.

Among the "relics" of Sheila Cassidy's imprisonment and torture is a shirt with a tear halfway down the front. The tear was made by her captors when she failed to remove her clothes at their command. Years later, reflecting on "The Way of the Cross" in the London *Tablet*, she observes how nakedness opens us not just to the whip or the electrode but also to the emotional assault of humiliation.

She writes, "When people are stripped they are somehow distanced, different from those with clothes. I believe this is one of the things that makes it possible for one person to torture another."[1]

In time, Cassidy was able to forgive the mindless abusers who reduced her to an object, denying her humanity. But of the drunken guards who, before Cassidy's arrival, raped every woman in the prison, she says, "Father forgive them...because I am not able."[2]

Released after a long period in solitary confinement, Cassidy returned to England, entered a contemplative order and later took up her profession again as medical director of a hospice. Her own suffering, deeply integrated through a life of prayer, has made her a compassionate tender of the dying. She is especially conscious of and sensitive to the unclothed patient who is fearful or angry at the "infantile state" to which he or she has been reduced.

Sheila Cassidy has gained new insight into Saint Irenaeus's dictum that "the glory of God is a human being fully alive." She believes that Irenaeus may well have been thinking not of a healthy, robust Christian but of "the countless broken Christ figures letting go of life."[3]

By her example, she calls us to a profound respect for the

human body in which Christ makes his home.

REFLECT

♦ In what ways have I been stripped? How have these experiences affected me?

♦ In what ways do I agree with (or can I expand on) Sheila Cassidy's insights in this reflection?

♦ How might my faith community make others aware (including those in the medical and correctional professions) of the need to respect the human body as the house of God? What can we do to stop torture and physical abuse throughout the world?

♦

[Job] said, "Naked I came from my mother's womb, and naked shall I return there; the LORD gave, and the LORD has taken away; blessed be the name of the LORD." (Job 1:21)

"But if God so clothes the grass of the field, which is alive today and tomorrow is thrown into the oven, will he not much more clothe you—you of little faith?" (Matthew 6:30)

THE WAY OF JESUS

They have reached the Place of the Skull. It is outside the city, just as it is beyond the boundaries within which the humanity of every person, Roman or Jew, Greek or African, Asian or Turk is recognized. Golgotha is the killing place. Here criminals, political dissidents and innocents alike are disposed of with a dispatch born of long experience. Crucifixion has served both the Carthaginians and Romans well as an instrument of capital punishment.

Several upright beams are already in place, like permanent mourners on cruelty's stage. An involuntary shudder runs through the prisoner as he sees that each beam has a rough peg in the middle. On that "seat" the victim half-sits as his limbs and torso gradually turn to lead. Jesus looks away rather than feed the gnawing predator known as anxiety.

The procession comes to a halt and the Cyrenean is instructed to lay down the crossbeam. "You have served your purpose," the captain of the guard tells him. "Now go your way." Simon turns to let the prisoner know, by his expression, that he is not abandoning him. He moves off just far enough to be absorbed into the first ranks of milling bystanders.

"Strip him."

The captain's tone is noncommittal. He has no particular interest in exposing this prisoner to the curiosity of the crowd. The condemned are always stripped naked, their clothing given to the guards. No exceptions are made—not even for one who has been identified as the King of the Jews.

Jesus feels his outer tunic of white wool being drawn up over his head, aggravating the wounds made by the thorns. He remembers how, as a boy, he had loved this peeling off of clothing as a prelude to cavorting around the house like a frisky lamb or bathing at the end of a blistering day.

He remembers his mother's gentle hands and the sight of her at the spindle. Every tunic or mantle he has ever worn has borne witness to her skill. Mary, like the provident wife extolled in Scripture, made garments and coverlets of enviable quality. Focusing on that image of her, Jesus recites a verse within himself: "Strength and dignity are her clothing,/ and she laughs at the time to come."[4] Would he too be able to laugh at the days to come? "Let it be," he prays.

As his inner tunic is pulled away, Jesus makes no attempt to cover himself. He knows the goodness of his body. He is grateful for the joys it has given him: swimming in the Jordan, dancing at the wedding in Cana, walking through the Judean hills, picking wildflowers for Martha and Mary, hoisting toddlers up on his shoulders, embracing Magdalene and John the Baptist, rowing a boat and casting a net with Peter and Andrew, standing tall in the synagogue to open the scroll and proclaim, "The Spirit of the Lord is upon me."[5]

An act intended for humiliation is transformed into a revelation. By accepting his nakedness, Jesus reminds those who have eyes to see that the human body reflects the divine image. When God created the first male and female, did not God gaze on them in the flesh and pronounce them very good? They had no need of garments, for there was nothing for them to fear or hide.

Jesus thanks God for his body and apologizes to it for the suffering it is about to bear.

REFLECT AND INTEGRATE

♦ How does this Tenth Station challenge me to relate to my own body and to the bodies of others?

♦ In what ways will I cherish my body and teach children to do likewise?

♦ How can we as a family or faith community become advocates for respect of the human body in advertising, film, TV and other media? Why is this a significant ministry in our time?

PRAYER OF ACTION

Jesus,
you
would
not
allow
evil
to turn
your own
nakedness
against
you.
Teach us to honor this humble house of flesh in
which
God
is
at
home
and
we are
garbed
in
spirit-
strength
and
dignity.

In response, I (we) will....

[1] Sheila Cassidy, "Christ the Fireman," *The Tablet*, April 17, 1993, p. 458.

[2] Sheila Cassidy, "The Way of the Cross," *The Tablet*, April 21, 1990, p. 475.

[3] Cassidy, "Christ the Fireman," p. 458.

[4] Proverbs 31:25.

[5] Luke 4:18a.

• XI •
CONFRONT
THE FEAR
Jesus Is Nailed to the Cross

Pain is the teacher
whose class we all try to avoid.
Yet there's no way to graduate
without passing her required course.

OUR WAY

The commandment Jesus repeats most often in the Gospels is
not "Love your neighbor" but "Do not be afraid." Seventeen
times in the Good News according to Matthew, Mark, Luke and
John, Jesus commands his disciples to "Fear not." He knew
them—as he knows us—better than anyone. His counsel is
aimed at the primal depths in each of us, those murky depths
wherein certain illegitimate creatures can remain hidden for a
lifetime.

Consider Peter. Like many Maine fishermen, he probably
did not know how to swim. But the sea was his familiar. He
could not have supported his family by harvesting lake sardines
and eels if he had been intimidated by the specter of drowning.

One night when he and his friends are caught in a sudden
storm, the entire crew is nearly paralyzed with terror. Then a
"ghost" walks toward them on the water and a familiar voice
says, "Take heart, it is I; do not be afraid."[1]

Peter promptly obeys. He rises above the terror like a buoy

bobbing above the waves. Instead of begging for shelter, he says, "Command me to come to you on the water."[2] Like a mother whose child is learning to ride a bike without its training wheels, Jesus encourages Peter to come ahead.

And all goes well until Peter remembers that he is "only human" and has never before walked on water. He drops the lifeline of faith, succumbs to fear and has to be saved by Jesus, who makes no effort to hide his own disappointment. The Lord's chastisement of Peter effectively means, "Why did you let fear squeeze the life out of you when you knew I was right here with you?"

No one can walk the way of Jesus without first taking that very question to heart.

"Whenever things go wrong in society, in a person's psyche, or in one's spiritual life," writes Brother David Steindl-Rast, "we may be sure that fear in one form or another lies at the root of the trouble."[3]

That insight gives me pause. What do I fear?

I fear the ugly face of violence, alcoholism and drug addiction in American society. My fear robs me of trust and hope. It inflicts the monotone pain of deadly skepticism that says, "Things have gone too far. No one can stop it now."

I fear the psychic loss of those whose love cloaks me against the pain of rejection, failure and "unneededness" (my husband and son, my parents and grandchildren). My fear drives me to play God by overprotecting these vital ones and trying to redirect their lives into safer pastures.

I fear the physical pain of cancer and the battle against it. I dread the possibility of a car accident in which I or a loved one might be mangled but not killed.

More than anything I fear being deprived for even one moment of fear's opposite. Richard Rohr, O.F.M., says it well: "A Christian is a person who has the freedom to feel the pain that's part of being human."[4]

Jesus, you confident water-walker, awaken me each day with the command I most often fail to obey: "Take heart; it is I. Do not be afraid. Pain is passing. Do not be afraid. Take heart."

REFLECT

◆ In what ways does fear lie at the root of my troubles?

◆ How have I overcome (or do I hope to overcome) my fear of pain?

◆ How can my faith community help people to "take heart" in our violence-plagued society?

◆

Even though I walk through the darkest valley,
   I fear no evil;
for you are with me.... (Psalm 23:4a-c)

There they crucified him, and with him two others, one on either side, with Jesus between them. (John 19:18)

THE WAY OF JESUS

For the first time, the prisoner learns that two others are to share his fate. They are thieves whose trade has proven traitorous. The younger one is new to the path of criminality. But Roman justice affords him the same punishment as his more experienced mentor. They have already been nailed to the crossbeams, and their screams course through the crowd, arousing some to perverse pleasure and others to commiseration.

Jesus prays for them as his own arms are stretched from one end of the beam to the other. His life has prepared him for this moment. He has known the pain of being cut by an errant saw, the knife of hunger in the belly, the burden of timber too heavy for his shoulders.

His mind and heart have been seasoned by rejection, eviction and the bullheaded enmity of those who should have been his strongest supporters. The Son of God has not been spared the pain that afflicts humanity. Nor is fear itself completely unknown to him. Did he not sweat blood in Gethsemane and grapple with the terror of crucifixion?

Concentrating on his prayer for the two who are now suspended from T-shaped crosses, Jesus does not see the swing of the soldier's hammer before it meets the nail that is even now piercing his right wrist. Blood gushes from the wound as the nail is implanted in the wood.

For a few seconds, his mind is blank. He is not aware of pain or of the executioner's shadow over his left arm. As the second nail is driven, the face and hands of Jesus are contorted.

He remains conscious as a fire rages through his upper body, cauterizing with mad intensity. The guards wonder at his silence, for they have not cut their teeth on the unyielding Hebrew prophets.

From her station on the edge of the crowd, Mary becomes the voice of her Son.

But he was wounded for our transgressions,
    crushed for our iniquities;
...and by his bruises we are healed.
    ...[Y]et he did not open his mouth;
like a lamb that is led to the slaughter....
[S]tricken for the transgression of my people.
(Isaiah 53:5, 7b, c, 8d)

She prays with her tired arms aloft, her face bathed in the tears her Son cannot allow himself. She groans as though in labor, for she is once again giving Emmanuel to a world that knows him not. "Be his strength, God of our ancestors!" she pleads. "Enable him to achieve the purpose for which you sent him."

Pain roars in his ears like a wild boar as the stake is driven through his feet and the crossbeam is attached to the upright beam set between the two thieves. Ropes are added to prevent his body from breaking loose. Jesus has lost all memory of his body before the piercing. He is the lamb raised on the altar of sacrifice.

Forty days in the desert had left him unacquainted with the kind of thirst that now devastates him. When a soldier presses a sponge permeated with wine and myrrh to Jesus' lips, he tastes but does not drink.

When the younger thief, fearful of what awaits him beyond the Romans' reach, hears his partner reviling Jesus, he gasps for breath to redeem himself. This repentant thief castigates the other's failure to "fear God" at the portal of death. Admitting their guilt and the innocence of the one strung up between them, the thief turns to Jesus and asks, in all humility, to be remembered "when you come into your kingdom."[5]

Jesus looks on him with love and says, "[T]oday you will be with me in Paradise."[6]

REFLECT AND INTEGRATE

◆ In what ways will this Eleventh Station serve as my icon when I am called to confront pain that cannot be avoided?

◆ How might my family or faith community minister, as the repentant thief did, to those in chronic, severe or terminal pain?

PRAYER OF ACTION

Jesus,
nailed
and
torn,
scourged
and
swollen,
you refuse the terror that catapults us
into betrayal or a precipitous death.
Your
blood,
Lion
of
Judah,
fortifies
our
courage.

In response, I (we) will....

[1] Matthew 14:27b.

[2] Matthew 14:28c.

[3] David Steindl-Rast, *Gratefulness, the Heart of Prayer: An Approach to Life in Fullness* (New York: Paulist Press, 1984), p. 199.

[4] Rohr, p. 145.

[5] Luke 23:42b.

[6] Luke 23:43c.

LETTING GO
Jesus Dies On the Cross

Are there Christians
who pray each day
from noon to three,
knowing that crucifixion
is both past and present?

OUR WAY

Giving birth is a way of dying. I've only done it once and I did not do it well. But the circumstances (delivery in a military hospital with crisp personnel who wanted to be elsewhere on Christmas night) enable me to see the analogy. I was less a willing participant than a prisoner whose body was subjected to the will of others.

Had Jesus been speaking to a woman rather than Peter that post-resurrection morning on the beach (see John 21:18), he might have said, "But when your labor begins, you will stretch out your body and someone else will hold you down and take you where you don't want to go." To conceptualize a painful death that gives life to others and glory to God, Jesus could not have offered a better analogy to his women disciples.

Some of his male followers would have understood as well. After meditating on the crucifixion, Saint Anselm observes:

Truly, Lord, you are a mother.... If you had not been in
labor, you could not have borne death; and if you had
not died, you would not have brought forth.[1]

Enduring a child custody case is a kind of dying. I've only done it once as a participant once removed (grandparent rather than parent). And I did not do it well. But the circumstances were so like those suffered by others that I know the analogy stands.

There is a death of trust. The afflicted parent and spouse is repeatedly subjected to unexpected blows—not from an enemy but from one who has been embraced as the most intimate friend. "I can't believe he (she) is doing this to me," the aggrieved one utters over and over like a child being drilled with an inexplicable lesson. "He (she) knows how much our child loves and needs me."

There is a death of credibility. I believed the justice system professionals who theorized about the court's commitment to protect "the child's inalienable right to a relationship with both parents." I believed that shared custody meant "comparable custody." And I believed that judges cared enough and were competent enough to extricate the truth from the tangle of conflicting testimony.

There is a death of hope. After two or three years, the day comes when the parent or grandparent is nailed to the reality of a broken relationship. My grandchild is growing up in a world made small by half. One equal side of her family tree has withered for want of the sunshine of her presence more than a few weeks a year.

When his disciples tried to prevent the children from visiting with Jesus, he set them straight in no uncertain terms: "Let the little children come to me, and do not stop them; for it is to such as these that the kingdom of heaven belongs."[2] Had Jesus been a grandparent, he would have said it more strongly.

There is only one crucifixion by which all are redeemed. But God alone knows how many crucifixions of body, heart and mind occur each hour. God alone counts the nails driven

each day into the flesh of the widowed, the orphaned, the
abused and victimized, the homeless, the hungry, the addicted
and criminalized, the war-torn, the disabled, the alienated and
ostracized.

Where is the justice in all this dying?

Maybe we've shackled ourselves to the wrong question.

On the cross, Jesus never says, "I can't stand any more of
this terrible injustice!" He says instead, "They do not know
what they are doing."[3]

In his play *J.B.*, Archibald MacLeish pictures Job's wife
asking her husband, "You wanted justice didn't you? There
isn't any—there is only love."

REFLECT

♦ What do I know in my flesh, heart or mind of crucifixion?

♦ How does the advice of J.B.'s wife apply in my life?

♦ How can we as a faith community help ourselves and others
to let go when letting go is all God has given us to do?

♦

Do not be far from me
  for trouble is near
  and there is no one to help. (Psalm 22:11)

Then Jesus, crying with a loud voice, said, "Father, into your
hands I commend my spirit." Having said this, he breathed his
last. (Luke 23:46)

THE WAY OF JESUS

He cannot remember his life before the pain began. That refuge
has been taken from him.

Bereft and bleeding, he has become "prey for jackals," "a
worm, and not human."[4]

To come to himself, he must escape, for a few moments at a
time, the clawing, the tearing and the dying.

He follows the sound of weeping and sees, at the foot of the
cross, his mother, Magdalene, Mary and John. Out of his
terrible deprivation, he will provide.

"Woman, here is your son." Then he said to the
  disciple, "Here is your mother."[5]
The jackals drag him down again before he has the consolation
of seeing the two clinging to one another, resisting the tide of
despair.

He had not known it would be like this. He is beyond help
in a land so desolate not even his Father inhabits it.

His lion's heart nearly breaks his ribs as he cries out, "My
God, my God, why have you forsaken me?"[6] There is no
answer, no absolute surety. Jesus cries out once again and lets
go.

Silence.

REFLECT AND INTEGRATE

♦ Henri Nouwen tells the story of two trapeze artists in a German circus.[7] The one who flies through the air explains that he must have absolute trust in the one who catches him. The act works perfectly because "the flyer does nothing and the catcher everything!" If the flyer were to grab the catcher, broken wrists might result. Reflecting on the way Jesus commends himself to the Father, Nouwen writes, "Dying is trusting in the Catcher!"

♦ How will I try to live so that in dying I can "trust the Catcher"?

♦ In what ways will we as a faith community minister to the dying and to those for whom there is no relief?

PRAYER OF ACTION

Jesus,
Lamb
of
sacrifice,
stumbling-
block
to the
self-willed,
lover of sinners, vindicator of the nonviolent,
mother in labor on bed of bloodstained wood,
we
venerate
you
in
every
least
one
likewise
nailed
to
present
rood.

In response, I (we) will....

XII. ♦ Letting Go

[1] Saint Anselm, *Prayers and Meditations of St. Anselm.* Translated by Benedicta Ward (New York: Penguin, 1979), p. 152.

[2] Matthew 19:14b.

[3] Luke 23:34c.

[4] See Psalm 63:10; 22:6.

[5] John 19:26b-27a.

[6] Mark 15:34c; see Psalm 22:1a.

[7] Henri Nouwen, *Our Greatest Gift: A Meditation on Dying and Caring* (London: Hodder & Stoughton, Ltd., 1994).

✦ XIII ✦
KEEPING VIGIL
Jesus Is Taken Down
From the Cross

After the death
of a loved one,
we let down, go flat,
feel, "It is finished."
But the vigil is
just beginning.

OUR WAY

I wasn't there when Leonard died at nine on Easter morning.
He was in a hospital in Cincinnati; I, a church in western
Maine. The vigil had been shared by his fellow friars, relatives
and friends—women and men whose lives bear the traces of his
good counsel.

A Franciscan for sixty-three years, Leonard invested his
talents with the skill of a herring fisherman who never comes
home with an empty net. He was a teacher, mentor and author
whose voice (part Dad, part friend) reached millions of readers
through books like *Saint of the Day* and *Believing in Jesus*. His
friend Patti Normile reported that Father Foley asked for his
writing materials from his hospital bed a day or two before he
died of cancer.

The first time I saw him, his wheelchair was parked at the
friars' dining table at the St. Francis Center for Peace and

Renewal. He looked me over with frank curiosity as though studying a bird not native to his region.

Sensing my discomfort (there were no other women in the room at the time), he reached out to take my hand and said, "Come in, come in. Grab yourself some food and sit right there where I can see you." That was the beginning of a four-month friendship that both of us felt had been there all along. Later I sent him a quote from Thomas Merton writing to his friend Boris Pasternak: "It is as if we met on a deeper level of life on which individuals are not separate beings...it is as if we were known to one another in God."[1]

When I began to bubble on about a new series of retreat books I would be editing, Leonard said bluntly, "I have nothing to do. No thing to do." Knowing that he had had surgery and seemed to be in remission, I replied, "Oh yes you do. You're going to write the book on John XXIII. You're just the man that can do it."

He immediately began plying me with questions, avid as a traveler set loose in a country he has not yet explored. Leonard was ready to roll. The next day he lit into a pile of John XXIII resources, taking notes and reflecting on what that greathearted shepherd would want to say to retreatants today.

We corresponded as regularly as we could—he restricted by his health, I by my workload. Assured by Brother Kevin that the book project was "keeping Leonard going," I cheered my friend on while assuring him that he need not worry. Other hands would be there to complete the project if he could not. He, in turn, kept me going by saying, "Has anyone told you lately what a good writer you are? Such detail! I'm a generalist—'just the abstractions, ma'am.'"

When his health deteriorated, we spoke once on the phone. He sounded disoriented and called me Barbara. I had asked him to send me a photo of himself. He responded, "Do you want the formal one from the official files or the crafty one?" Naturally, I requested the crafty one. His memory became fogbound and I did not receive a picture until our managing editor sent me his memorial card a few weeks later. (Was that the crafty one, Leonard? It looks greathearted to me.)

On that brief January visit to Cincinnati, it dawned on me just in time that Leonard was more than a fellow author and a sudden friend. He was a priest, formed in the gospel life-style of Francis of Assisi. I made my confession to him in his room and wept at the simplicity of his counsel. The only penance he could bring himself to give me was "Take a nap."

I wasn't there to hold his hand when he died. But there are many ways of keeping vigil with those whom a loving God has placed in our path, saying, "Attend to this one." Nor does the vigil end when the other moves on. As he looks down at me from the bulletin board above my desk, Leonard makes it clear that he is praying for me and trusts that I'm doing the same for him.

I am reminded of a darkened church on a Holy Thursday night in which we, the assembly of believers, chanted over and over in hushed voices, "Stay with me. Remain here with me. Watch and pray...."[2]

REFLECT

♦ How have I kept vigil with others?

♦ In what ways do I feel called to hearken to the needs of those God has placed in my path?

♦ What is our vision of a faith community that "stays awake" in a world that often seems oblivious to the sick, the dying, those in mourning?

I commune with my heart in the night;
I meditate and search my spirit.... (Psalm 77:6)

Blessed are those who mourn, for they will be comforted.
(Matthew 5:4)

THE WAY OF JESUS

The Jews have requested that the three crucified men be
removed before the sabbath begins. To dispatch the two thieves
more quickly, the soldiers break their legs. But there is no need
to do likewise to the one whose cross bears the sign "King of
the Jews." He has given up his life of his own accord. A Roman
in need of certainty, considering the charges of treason and
rebellion against the state, thrusts his lance into the side of
Jesus "and at once blood and water came out."[3]

Having hidden his discipleship while Jesus was alive,
Joseph of Arimathea now gathers the courage to show his
allegiance. He petitions Pilate for the body, and the procurator
agrees. Joseph and a few other disciples liberate Jesus from the
nails and ropes, handing him down to his mother and the other
women.

Mary holds her Son on her lap as though he were again a
boy she would comfort after a fall. She rocks back and forth
like a rabbi laboring to bring down God's mercy on the crushed
ones. Magdalene and the other Mary reverence his wounded
hands, kiss his feet, wash him with their tears.

Joseph and John stand back a little, respectful of the
women's prerogative as mourners and as disciples not found
wanting in these last days. John weeps quietly, without shame.
His companion is tortured by guilt for failing to declare himself
a believer before his peers in the Sanhedrin. His anger at
himself temporarily mitigates his grief.

When Nicodemus arrives bearing a king's quantity of

myrrh and aloes, he ministers to all the mourners by requiring
them to assist in preparing the body. Magdalene carefully
removes the crown of thorns, while Mary repeatedly pushes the
disheveled hair away from her Son's face. "Sleep, my Son," she
says, closing his somber eyes. "Sleep."

Removing the body to a nearby garden, the company of
mourners prepares the spices and burial cloths. Each makes
sure that the other shares in the privilege of washing the body
that has borne the scourge, the thorn, the crossbeam and the
nails. They then anoint Jesus with oil, smoothing it over his
entire body.

Remembering the repentant woman at the house of Simon
the Pharisee, John observes, "He was so touched by the manner
in which she anointed him—as though she fathomed the
mystery in him that we could not force ourselves to look at. He
assured her that, because she loved so liberally, she would be
forgiven everything."

As Magdalene wraps the hands and feet of Jesus in soft
linen bands, she recalls how tenderly he had washed the feet of
the disciples at the paschal supper. "If we want him to live on in
us," she says, "we must be as willing to mother the lepers and
the tax collectors, the beggars and the prostitutes as he was.
Otherwise, we are not worthy of him." At this she breaks into
sobs and cannot be comforted.

Nicodemus has brought a simple tunic of his own in which
to garb the King of the Jews. He might well have brought a silk
mantle, but he refrained out of respect for Jesus' royal poverty.
The two Marys work together, packing the myrrh and aloes into
every fold of the garment until the body is richly scented.

His mother remembers how he loved the springtime aroma
of lilies and wild roses, how he relished the perfume of cedar
and of newly-crushed grapes. She places her hand lightly on her
dead son's chest and recites under her breath, "[T]he scent of

your garments is like the scent of Lebanon."[4]

Now all join in wrapping the redolent body in yards of winding sheets, moving slowly like priests before the Ark of the Covenant. Finally they wrap the head of Jesus, the head of the warrior victorious in battle. Mary's heart is pierced by the sight. (She wrapped him in swaddling clothes and laid him in a tomb.)

The mourners huddle over the body as though shielding him from the evening breezes. Sensing that they are not yet ready to take the next step, John begins to tell the story of Lazarus of Bethany. When he comes to the part about Lazarus hobbling out, wound hand and foot in his burial cloths, everyone laughs at the comic relief.

"Untie him and let him go," Mary says, hope rising, an eagle above a sepulcher.

They stand, keeping vigil for his sake and their own.

REFLECT AND INTEGRATE

♦ In what ways does the Thirteenth Station inspire me to comfort the mourning?

♦ What can our faith community do to minister to bereaved families before, during and after a funeral?

♦ How are we as Christians called to keep vigil with those made homeless, orphaned or widowed, disabled or hopeless by their experience of war?

PRAYER OF ACTION

Jesus,
your
house
is
dark,
your
windows
shut.
We gasp and falter, desperate for a single
sustaining breath from you.
Will
these
wounds
ever
heal?
These
ears
ever
hearken?

In response, I (we) will....

[1] Merton, *The Courage for Truth*, p. 87.

[2] "Stay With Me," #170 in *Gather,* ©1984, Les Presses de Taizé, GIA Publications, Inc., agent.

[3] John 19:34b.

[4] Song of Songs 4:11.

· XIV ·
BREAKING FREE
Jesus Is Entombed

When a doctor awakened
from a twenty-three-day coma,
he uttered a single word: "Yes."

OUR WAY

There are ways in which we as Catholics are wound and bound
and locked up in the tomb. Resurrection happens every day.
Jesus is there, breaking free. But we are laid out. We are
hanging around in the tomb of spiritual stagnation, waiting for
God or others to answer our prayers.

And what are we praying for?

I'll "be little" and speak only for myself and a few friends,
fellow catechists and sister seekers. We may be more
representative than we know.

We pray for a Church in which every Catholic in every
parish will break out of the tomb of insularity, throw off the
binding cloths of shyness or exclusivity or dated piety and hold
out both hands in welcome.

Like Abram and Sarai, many Catholics are nomads. We
don't belong to the parish where our grandparents had their
own pew, or even the parish where everyone knew our parents'
names. Every five or ten years, we have to work our way into a
new parish. Those of us whose jobs or ministries require us to
travel have to worship repeatedly in "strange lands" where the
official sign of peace is the only greeting we receive. How are

we Catholics in the United States, whose very name is
"All-Inclusive," ever going to assimilate the refugees and all
those from afar whose first language is other than English, if
we haven't yet learned how to welcome each other?

We pray for a profound understanding of the advice in
Hebrews: "Do not neglect to show hospitality to strangers, for
by doing that some have entertained angels without knowing it"
(13:2).

We pray too for a Church in which every Catholic in every
parish will break out of the tomb of the caste system which
allows the Spirit's gifts, given freely without benefit of official
sanction, to be stifled, denied or shelved. In our vineyard, too
many grapes remain unharvested while people lack authentic
preaching, spiritual formation and even the Eucharist itself in
those places where ordained celibate males are not available.

My friends and I pray for a profound understanding of
Paul's advice: "...[T]he members of the body that seem to be
weaker are indispensable, and those members of the body that
we think are less honorable we clothe with greater honor, and
our less respectable members are treated with greater respect"
(1 Corinthians 12:22b-23).

Let those who have the proven gift of leadership lead; the
gift of healing, heal; the gift of teaching, teach; the gift of
preaching, preach; the gift of counseling, counsel; the gift of
political wisdom, govern; the gift of prophecy, speak out. Let
no gift of the Spirit run dry because it is manifested in one who
is considered weaker, less honorable or less respectable.

Finally, we pray for a Church in which every Catholic in
every parish will break out of the tomb of cultural insularity
that prevents us from freely sharing our own treasure while
closing our minds to the truths cherished by other religions.
Speaking of Hinduism, Buddhism, Islam and other "non-
Christian religions," Vatican II says, "The Catholic Church

rejects nothing which is true and holy in these religions."[1]

Ours is an exalted faith tradition. We are flawed but beautiful in our sacramental rituals (marking every significant human passage from birth to death), in our companionship with the saints (making us humbly proud of our older sisters and brothers, Francis of Assisi, Teresa of Avila, Martin de Porres, Joan of Arc, Ignatius of Loyola, Kateri Tekakwitha of the Mohawks of New York, César Chavez of Arizona and California, Katherine Drexel of Philadelphia, Oscar Romero of El Salvador, Thea Bowman of Canton, Mississippi).

We rejoice in our affirmation of Mary as mother and disciple, our esteem for human life, our schools in which gospel values are not hidden under a bushel basket, our incarnational habit of finding God wherever we look (in creation, in the arts and sciences, in ethnic cultures both mainstream and oddball, in our claiming every day as holy ground by welding our lives to Christ's in the liturgical year, even—God help us!—in the media).

At this final Station, we commit ourselves to be "Resurrection witnesses"—and to raise others up as best we can.

REFLECT

♦ In what ways am I hanging around in the tomb, waiting for God or others to make things happen? Why?

♦ Do I share any of the above prayers for the Church? Which ones? What would I add?

♦ What commitment will we make to participate in the resurrection of our faith community—or our Church at large?

*...Thus says the LORD God: I am going to open your graves,
and bring you up from your graves, O my people; and I will
bring you back to the land of Israel. (Ezekiel 37:12b)*

*Now there was a garden in the place where he was crucified,
and in the garden there was a new tomb in which no one had
ever been laid. (John 19:41)*

THE WAY OF JESUS

It is evening on the day of preparation for the sabbath. The
companions of Jesus can no longer delay. His body must be
placed in the tomb provided by Joseph of Arimathea. The three
men—Joseph, John and Nicodemus—lift Jesus with great care,
like fathers entrusted for the first time with their newborn sons.
Slowly they raise his body to their shoulders as the women
form a solemn procession behind them.

Mary weeps silently, holding her head high with the dignity
of a royal mother and honored disciple. Magdalene and the
other Mary cry aloud, beating their breasts in the traditional
manner. They cannot bear the thought of leaving Jesus alone in
this cold stone house of the dead. "Rabboni! Rabboni!"
Magdalene wails, "Don't leave us!"

Inside the tomb, they place the swaddled body of their
loved one on a narrow platform carved into the wall. Darkness
veils their faces from one another, sparing them the sight of
another's sorrow. John can carry his own grief. But if he sees
the pain imprinted on Mary's face, he will give way.

Reaching within for communion with those who have
walked the way of sorrow before her, Mary hears a voice from
Lamentations:

Is it nothing to you, all you who pass by?
Look and see
if there is any sorrow like my sorrow....[2]

The time for hope and waiting will come again. But now she must experience her loss so that its redeeming power may be set free.

The companions stand in silence. Each strengthens the other by bodily witness. Together they are sustained by the witness of their Hebrew ancestors, a people formed by suffering and enslavement, sorrow and exile, hunger and thirst for the God of Abraham and Sarah, who is to be trusted. In their present deprivation, the mourners can make Job's words their own: "See, he will kill me yet will I trust in him" (13:15, *King James Version*).

John bows and turns to leave, placing a protective arm around Mary's shoulders. He treasures in his heart Jesus' legacy to him: "Behold your mother." Mary understands and clasps the hand of her "son." When all are ready, Joseph pushes the rounded stone set in a groove before the entrance of the cave. It rolls heavily into place, sealing the tomb.

Nicodemus lights a torch in the gathering darkness. His gesture is an eloquent testimony to the Teacher who said, "I am the light of the world. Whoever follows me will never walk in darkness but will have the light of life."[3]

Together the friends of Jesus make their way back into the city he had loved as his own. There, as a boy, he had taken his place among the elders in the Temple, astounding them with his knowledge of the Law. There he had communed with his disciples at the Paschal Supper, giving them bread blessed and broken, wine blessed and poured, saying "This is my body.... This is my blood."[4] And there, on Jerusalem's maternal breast, he had laid down his life for his friends.

"Jerusalem, Jerusalem," he had cried. "...I tell you, you will not see me again until you say, 'Blessed is the one who comes in the name of the Lord.' "[5]

The companions of Jesus, walking close together and

speaking quietly for security's sake, urge one another to take heart. The torch parts the night before them. "He is yet with us," Mary says.

REFLECT AND INTEGRATE

♦ How am I challenged by this final Station to a deeper faithfulness to Jesus, to my loved ones, to my faith community?

♦ What commitment will we make—as a family or as a community—to walk the Way of Jesus in sunlight and in shadow until death makes us one?

PRAYER OF ACTION

Jesus,
you
command
us,
"Do this
in
memory
of me."
Teach us how to be Eucharist for one another.
Embolden us to break free from the tomb of
self-
concern.
Enliven
our
dry bones.
Lead
us
home.

In response, I (we) will....

[1] *Declaration on the Relationship of the Church to Non-Christian Religions*, #2.

[2] Lamentations 1:12.

[3] John 8:12b-c.

[4] See Mark 14:22-24.

[5] Matthew 23:39.

EPILOGUE
He Is Risen! We Shall Rise!

The Way of the Cross is the way of life. It is a prayer that
makes disciples of us when we allow it to become more than an
in-house Lenten devotion. When we give ourselves to it, year
after year, it frees us from fear of death—and of life. It reshapes
our vision, enabling us to see with Job that "...there is hope for
a tree,/ if it is cut down, that it will sprout again" (14:7a).

I remember a Jesuit retreat director in upstate New York
telling us a story about Thomas Edison. My memory of the
details is inexact. But the narration went something like this:
Once a fire destroyed Edison's photo-finishing plant. The
whole thing burned to the ground. As soon as the fire was under
control, Edison began planning how to rebuild it.

In the rubble, one of his sons found a framed portrait of
Edison. The frame was blackened, but the photograph was
unharmed. Later Thomas A. presented the portrait to a friend.
On it he had inscribed, "Never touch me."

That is the message of the Way. At the Fourteenth Station,
resurrection is already breaking through. Jesus is not destroyed.
He gives up his life. And life is given back to him. So it is for
us, no matter what cancer or AIDS, abuse or alienation, divorce
or betrayal, bereavement or bankruptcy may do to us. "Never
touch me."

There is another message of the Way. It is one we need to
hear when we are healthy, physically fit, financially stable and
feeling right with God.

In *The Call of Stories: Teaching and the Moral*

Imagination, Robert Coles explores how compelling stories, if taken to heart, can be channels of grace. Among his examples is a story by Anton Chekhov called "Gooseberries."

The main character, Ivan Ivanych, muses on why, when he sees a happy person, he feels unaccountably oppressed. He imagines all the contented people in the world at that very moment. They are enjoying life (as though eating gooseberries one by one) without giving a thought to the millions who are suffering "behind the scenes."

Ivan Ivanych wonders how to awaken the contented ones from their "general hypnosis." His answer is memorable.

> Behind every door of every contented, happy man,
> there ought to be someone standing with a little
> hammer and continually reminding him with a knock
> that there are unhappy people, that however happy he
> may be, life will sooner or later show him its claws,
> and trouble will come to him—illness, poverty, losses,
> and then no one will see or hear him, just as he neither
> sees nor hears others.[1]

The Way of the Cross is the someone with a little hammer. If by the time we reach the Twelfth Station, we see only Jesus on the cross and remain oblivious to the raped widows of Bosnia-Hercegovina, the embittered paraplegic veterans of Vietnam, the mothers of the disappeared in South America, the slain missionaries in Liberia, the person in the next pew whose spouse or child died last week, the family next door whose breadwinner is an alcoholic, then we have not prayed it well.

We pray it well when we remember that his way is our way—the same all-inclusive *our* we mean when we pray "Our Father." And that way leads where he has gone before.

He is risen, alleluia! We shall rise. Alleluia, alleluia!

[1] Robert Coles, *The Call of Stories* (Boston: Houghton Mifflin, 1989), p. 195.